MOVEMENTS AND PUBLIC ADMINISTRATION

MOVEMENTS AND PUBLIC ADMINISTRATION

Editor

V. Bhaskara Rao

KALPAZ

Movements and Public Administration

ISBN : 978-81-7835-916-8

Published in 2012 in India by
Kalpaz Publications
C-30, Satyawati Nagar,
Delhi - 110052
E-mail: kalpaz@hotmail.com
Ph.: 9212729499

Lasser Type Setting : Rajender Vashist, Delhi
Printed at : Chawla Offset Printers, Delhi

In Memory

of

Prof. S.P. Verma

CONTENTS

PREFACE

The Constitution of India in Chapter III on Fundamental Rights and in Chapter IV on Directive Principles of State Policy committed to provide individual freedom and promised to protect the social justice. Accordingly, the Constitution created a number of independent agencies to protect the interests of scheduled castes and scheduled tribes, minority communities, women and other weaker sections. People belonging to these sections constitute more than 50 percent of the population of India. They are socially, culturally backward and about 40 per cent of them are economically below the poverty line.

The Parliament of India realised the particular and specific problems and interests of these people and enacted the necessary laws, formulated policies and made provisions, established institutions to carry out programmes for their upliftment in all the fields.

Public Administration at all levels of governments are expected to share the concern for ensuring responsive, accountable, decentralised and people friendly administration. Public administration must prove that it is there for the welfare of the people. It appears, this message has not been conveyed effectively by the bureaucracy and the administrative machinery.

Therefore, there is considerable dissatisfaction and frustration among the people, especially the weaker sections of the society about the indifference, irresponsiveness, apathy and lack of accountability of public administration. The people, particularly, the vulnarable groups are greatly concerned with law and order and the investigation of offences. Their faith in the delivery of prompt and proper justice has been considerably eroded.

Therefore, it is but natural for these people in a democracy to organise themselves utilising their rights to demand for welfare, social justice and empowerment.

In response to the people's demands, the government enacted certain laws like 73rd and 74th Amendments to the constitution, created Human Rights Commissions, allocated more budgetary provisions and extended more reservations in education and public employment.

Despite the Laws, programmes and allocations, many problems remained unsolved due to irresponsibility and inefficiency of public administration and corruption in politics and administration.

To achieve the rightful demands, the people started oganising agitations / movements on a regular scale and pressurising the politicians and the bureaucracy to yield to their demands. Peoples movements gained certain demands depending on their pressures adopted and the responses of the administration to provide relief to their demands.

The Constitution of India entrusted the public administration to assume the charge of the agent of social transformation. But the past experience shows a wide gap between the promise and performance. The governance in general moved against the interests of the common people. The new ideology of the state liberalisation, privatisation and globalization gave up the transformatory role of the governance. The process led to the emergence of violent peoples movements and a violent state. The positive, secular and the socialist nature of the state is gradually dying.

A number of studies have been made to understand and explain the phenomenon of the social movements in India by eminent sociologists, political scientists and economists, state institutions of research conducted surveys gave suggestions and recommendations. Despite efforts of research the problems persisted and continued to draw the attention of the public to realise the extent of the problems.

The New Public Administration Society of India organised its 4th Annual Conference in the Department of Public Administration and Human Resource Management, Kakatiya University, Warangal during 30-31 August 1999. The theme of the conference was "Peoples Movements and Public Administration". A large number of papers were presented on the Movements of women, SCs, STs, minorities, human rights, labour and environment. Eminent scholars from different universities in India participated. The papers were not published by any body. The Secretary-cum-Treasurer of New Public Administration Society of India, made an attempt to publish some of those papers. The first eight papers of this book along with other papers, were invited for this volume.

Prof. S.P. Verma has been the president of the New Public Administration Society of India. The papers are edited and the volume is dedicated to Prof. S.P. Verma to honour him for his service rendered to Public Administration discipline and the cause of New Public Administration Society of India.

I am greatful to all the colleagues in the department of Public Administration who hosted the conference. I thank all the paper writers and those who participated in the conference.

This volume will be useful to all the students, teachers of Public Administration and other activists of different peoples movements.

Warangal **V. Bhaskara Rao**

18-03-2011

LIST OF CONTRIBUTORS

1. **Prof. G. Haragopal**
   Department of Political Science,
   University of Hyderabad, Hyderabad.
2. **Prof. Alice Vidya Sagar**
   Department of Public Administration,
   Osmania University, Hyderabad - 500 007.
3. **Prof. R.K. Sapru**
   Department of Public Administration,
   Panjab University, Chandigarh.
4. **Prof. V. Bhaskara Rao**
   Department of Public Administration,
   Kakatiya University, Warangal - 506 009.
5. **Dr. T.V. Sujatha Kumari**
   Asst. Professor,
   Department of Public Administration,
   Kakatiya University, Warangal - 506 009.
6. **Dr. P. Veeraiah**
   Reader in Public Administration,
   Govt. College, Siddipet, A.P.
7. **Prof. S. Seshaiah**
   Department of Law,
   Sri Krishna Devaraya University, Ananthapur.

8. **Dr. Gunti Ravi**
Assistant. Professor,
Dr. B.R. Ambedkar Open University, Hyderabad.

9. **Dr. M. Venkat Reddy**
Assistant. Professor,
School of Distance Learning and Continuing Education, Warangal - 500 609

10. **Dr. A. Vijay Kumar**
Reader in Public Administraion,
Government Pingle Womens' College, Warangal.

11. **Prof. S.M. Rahamatullah**
Dean, School of Arts and Social Sciences,
and Prof. of Political Science and Public Administration,
Moulana Azad National Open University, Gachibowli, Hyderabad.

12. **Prof. Krishna K. Tummala**
Director,
Graduate Programme in Public Administration
Department of Political Science,
Kansas State University,
Manhattan, U.S.A.

13. **Prof. Srinibas Pathi**
Head, Department of Public Administration
Mizoram University,
AIZWAL.

14. **Prof. Ch. Balaramulu (Retired)**
Department of Public Administration and HRM,
Kakatiya University,
Warangal.

15. **Prof. P. Narasimha Rao**
Department of Public Administration and HRM,
Kakatiya University,
Warangal.

16. **Dr. V.V. Kanna**
Faculty Member,
Department of Public Administration and HRM,
Kakatiya University, Warangal.

17. **Dr. T. Yadagiri Rao**
Associate Professor,
Department of Public Administration and HRM,
Kakatiya University, Warangal.

18. **Dr. Devath Suresh**
Post - Doctoral Fellow,
Department of Public Administration & HRM,
Kakatiya University, Warangal.

1

ADMINISTRATIVE RESPONSE TO TRANSFORMATIVE MOVEMENTS

G. Haragopal

An examination of research on bureaucracy as well as experience, subjective and objective, reveals that the administrative system in India, by and large, is hostile to any assertion protest or organised movement by ordinary people. There are some individual exceptions where administrators in their personal capacity might have taken a sympathetic position on peoples movements. But there would be hardly any instance where the administrative system as a whole or in parts responded in a helpful way towards any transformative movement. This is more so with the police, the coercive wing of the administrative system. As this behavioural pattern seems to be a universal phenomenon, this needs deeper probing.

Analysis of hostile or adversial administrative response to peoples movements poses methodological and theoretical problems as it presupposes dichotomy of politics and administration. Is administrative response different from that of political as politics is both a source of power and legitimacy and also a search for alternative solutions to the chronic or emerging problems of the society ? In this paper, since the whole question cannot be resolved, it proceeds with an assumption that the administrative system has come to enjoy 'relative autonomy' in most of the developing countries including India. The relative autonomy is based on three premises :

One, the political classes have arrived at a consensus on the economic mode of development.

Two, different political parties are competing for a share in political power and are in search of alternative sources of legitimacy of power in a highly fluctuating balance of power.

Three, the administrative system representing the long range of interests of the dominant classes has come to enjoy relative autonomy, both in terms of articulating the interest of the rulers and in using institutionalised repressive force wherever or whenever there is a basic challenge to the model of development, structure of power and cultural dominance.

These premises are not ruling out politics *per se* what all that is being argued is that the administrative system which includes police, para-military and military has come to share the 'political' power and, therefore, cannot be treated as 'mare instrument' of power. Their sources of power are not only political class but information technology, technical expertise in addition to the command of organised force. This in fact is one of the offshoots of the declining political content of development and increasing techno - managerial backup. The declining capacity of the political system to organize and mobilize the masses for alternative solutions give rise to repression where the armed wing of administration acquires critical presence.

Based on the above hypothetical framework, one can look at the unfolding administrative responses to transformative movements.

A paper of this kind can start with a question : Why transformative movements come up in a given society ? An attempt to analyse this question can provide the necessary backdrop for a deeper grasp of the administrative response to transformative movements.

Every society at a given point of time inherits or develops its own inner mechanisms to keep the life move on. It has a form of production, channels of distribution, hegemonic ideology and institutional arrangement to continuously reproduce the system. If that given order is allowed to continue unquestioned, such a situation is characterised as "peaceful and orderly" and therefore a stable and lawful society. Any questioning or action against the system is not only characterised as anti-social, anti-people, but put down with force which can become ruthless. For such attempts to questions have the potential to cause changes or upset the existing balance of social forces. The measures to suppress such situations are characterised as socially desirable, rationally justifiable and legally tenable. The system makes no attempt to ask for the causes of unrest as it depends more on the force than a rational choice to deal with the basic question.

It is not recognised that the movements represent an intrinsic motion in the social progress. They emanate from two major sources:

1. The continuous struggles of human beings with the forces of nature.
2. Search for redefinition and restructuring of the relations between human beings.

The struggles of the human beings against nature both in terms of understanding the deeper laws that govern the forces of nature and applying that body of knowledge in furthering or bettering the human conditions is a perpetual source of change. In every situation where human enquiry succeeds, it not only alters the relationship of human beings with nature but calls for readjustment in social relations as both of them are organically interconnected. The change in material conditions either in the first phase of agrarian civilisation, or subsequent stage of agrarian changes through green revolution or industrial revolution, electronic revolution or information revolution, did carry serious implications to the moral value's framework at one level and attitudinal patterns at another level. Marx, while exploring the laws of motion, believed that changes in material conditions occur at a faster rate than changes in social relations. They, in a way, do not correspond to the objective material conditions on one to one basis calling for conscious effort to restructure the relationships. It is progress in conscious effort that takes the form of movements. It appears that while the change in nature human relationship is a lesser painful process, the change in the nature of social relationships is far more complex and painful. Therefore the modes of articulation of change are varied and multi layered. Grasping the intensity and magnitude of any given movement can always be problematic calling for deeper insights, better analytical tools, methodological rigor and comprehensive empirical observation and data.

The modes of articulation of movements range from individual anger to violent outburst of a group to protracted struggles. It is the range of the manifestations that gives rise to not only varied interpretations but even to diametrically opposite conceptualisation. The two major paradigms in social knowledge—one emphasising that societies are in search of equilibrium and the other perceiving a perpetual motion—is an example of this epistomic dilemma.

The multilayered nature and levels of protest give rise to equally varied responses. In Indian context, this could be seen in the range of the on going movements. These are at a milder level non-violent protests, demonstrations, representations, appeals to moral sensibilities and so on. Pamphleteering, dharnas, indefinite or relay hunger strikes opposite to the Secretariat or the Assembly in any part of the country can be a testimony to the constant but slow motion in the social process of seeking redressal within the given structure of relationships. These movements can be called as 'incremental movements'.

These are movements of the farmers, government

employees, industrial worhers, rural poor, slum dwellers which take sometimes, aggressive forms involving bandh calls or physical action damaging the property, attacks on adversarial groups. There have been prolonged strikes of the workers and employees, aggressive protestes by the dalits, women movement like anti - liquor struggle or famous protest against multi-national it happened in Karnataka.

There are also environmental movements like Chipco or Narmada Bachao Andolan or civil liberties and democratic rights movement organised fairly on a long terms basis. There is right to information movement having explosive potential. All these movements question the model of development or structuring of power but may not question the very basis of the total system. They could be characterised as reformistic in the sense that they are not satisfied with the existing arrangement but may not aim at alteration of the totality of the relations.

There are identity and autonomy movements at one level and the struggles of tribals, peasants, agrarian poor at another level. Some of these movements have assumed the form of armed struggles. These struggles for identity and autonomy aim, altering the basis of power relations and cultural specificity of the existing structure question, the very material basis and carry uncompromising struggle for a qualitative change in the totality of the relationships. All these movements could broadly be categorised as either militant or transformative movements.

III

The administrative response to the incremental demands is responsive in certain instances and that of indifference in certain other instances. A responsive administrative culture is conceivable only where the sensitivity and sensibility is quite high. An administrative system which is grounded in Weberian equilibrium centric parading can act and react in a rational way as its source of strength lies in its legal rational structure. The administrative systems of Indian kind is more rooted in the 'impersonal' approach to the people to the point of being totally indifferent. It responds to the demands of the powerful and the privileged but holds the poor and the powerless in utter contempt.

The incrementalist demands generate pyraveekars, middle men and rise of opportunistic and ambitious inviduals propelled by power impulse but not got accommodated in formal politics. If the 'agitating' groups fail to attract media attention and of a middle man, they get tired and reconcile with what life offers them. There are several instances where relay fasts for hundreds of days produce no response. The leaders or those who take up these demands, some times start with a threat of self-immolation, pledge for carrying out an uncompromising struggle and create a hue and cry. In fact, at the end when they fail to realize what they promise, such groups and their leaders desperately look for some face saving device or a pretext to get out of a very embarrassing situation. They even prefer getting arrested as an escape route and give up the demands.

It is widely noticed that in the recent past administrative indifference to incremental demands has been on an increase. This has led to enormous corruption as those who can afford to get the things done through other means. There are persons and groups who use their social and political or what may be called 'influential' linkages to neutralise this indifference. Those who are powerless and

have no linkages, give it up; but become 'agents' of cynicism. The social costs of administrative indifference is not only in terms of widespread frustration but provide greater justification to agitational and more aggressive forms of protest in a society.

The movements which are organised on a long term basis by the very articulate sections of the society do get better response of the state in general and administrative systems in particular. These movements also get considerable media support—national and international. For such pressure there are two types of responses; a) they lead to passing of a new legislation conceding the demands in principle or setting up of an institution. These institutions may be created through an executive order or a creation of autonomous or semi-autonomous institutions by an act of parliament or state legislation.

There are several examples of such response. The creation of Commissions for scheduled castes and scheduled tribes or Commission for women and minorities and so on. The creation of National Human Rights Commission is one such significant evidence. There are several legislations protecting the rights of the vulnerable sections. The extension of reservations to the backward classes or attempt to extend political reservations for women or imposition of prohibition or preparation of a bill for Right to Information are a part of this process. These responses are, no doubt, a gain to the agitating groups and do make some difference to the balance of power and structure of relationship. However, the working of the institutions and enforcement of the legislations depends more on the depth of the movement and its continued sustenance and possibility of its revival at one level and the administrative commitment to the new treasure at another level.

IV

The crucial parts or the turning point in the discourse on administrative response is its behaviour towards the militant or transformative movements. These movements are rooted in the belief or conviction that the human problems at a given point of time are located in the existing structure and have got to be solved through human agency. Any amount of effort to improve the system is of no avail as the source of the problem is the structure itself. They also believe that it is within human capacity to build alternative systems in terms of restructuring of power relations and reduction of cultural hegemony. The class struggles further maintain that the material basis on which social relations rest can be radically altered through the struggles of the oppressed. It is these movements which pose a serious challenge to the system as a whole and specifically the administrative system which stands face to face with the movements.

These movements are essentially political in scope and content. In a normal situation they should be tackeled politically in the sense of counter mobilisation or very comprehensive package of changes which in turn could involve surrender of privilege and sharing of power, if not transfer of power from the privileged to the most disadvantaged. A political system meant for protecting and promoting the interests of certain sections will be in no position to concede such alteration. Faced with opposites, the administrative system is called upon to negotiate with a complex context. Complex in the sense that the administrative system which is essentially meant for maintaining the equilibrium of social forces has to handle a new situation calling for higher capabilities and new modes of mediation with the forces that continuously get emanated from the disequilibrium. In the history of administration there are neither many such instances nor evidences where the administrative system could successfully handle such 'unexpected' or 'unanticipated' changes.

It is also quite evident that the existing political system, neither prepared nor willing to politically respond, becomes dependent to start on civil administration but ultimately on organised coercive force. These developments have very serious implications for administrative theory and practice.

Max Weber 'romanticised' bureaucracy because of its location in the legal rational authority. The rules, regulations, procedures, impersonal norms which are central to his construction get almost abandoned in the context under discussion. There are administrators – civil and non-civil – who maintain that extra ordinary situations calls for extra ordinary responses. This extra ordinary response often means arming the administrative system with repressive laws to the point of allowing the administrative system arbitrary exercise of power. The logic of the rule of law in terms of regulation of organised force starts collapsing. This could be logical but the question remains that how can the arbitrary use of forces by itself can be the source of legitimacy? That is akin to the 'unrestrained freedom' that men were supposed to have enjoyed 'in the state of nature' where force mediated all forms of relations. This context exposes the administrative system and the partisan interests that it represents. Although there is a continuous argument that force is used in the interest of common good of the people, the argument cannot stand any rational scrutiny. If the large mass of people form the social base of power, it should be possible to govern through rule of law and also political counter-mobilisation of people. This is not to argue that the transformative movements always enjoy conscious mass support; their strength, however, lies more with the fundamental questions they raise about the structure of relationships than their mass base. There are several instances where the quantium of force used by administration is far higher than the concrete situation calls for. Instead of answering the questions and acting upon them, they resort to stifling of the question itself. Thus situation gets aggravated giving rise to a vicious circle. The ultimate 'arbitrary repressive power', undoubtedly, indicates not the strength but the crisis of the governance.

The political elite, as stated earlier-gradually cause to be the source of solutioin to othe problems and therefore cause to be the source of legitimacy of power. Given their political incapacity, the administrative system – better organised and armed – starts occupying the "political space". It is this process that leads to relative autonomy of the administrative system. The momentum that the relative autonomy gains, inevitably moves towards what one may call from a position of autonomy to a position of 'autonomous'. The political elites are left with no option except co-opting or recruiting administrative officers including the police officers into the political process.

The relative autonomy gives rise to administrative characteristics which are a clear negation of all what Max Weber maintained in his concept of bureaucracy. For, relative autonomy and arbitrary power always go together. In the normal course, administrative system is accountable to the political level but under the new context, it is this arrangement that collapses. The normal controls exercised by the civil over police not only crumble but the control mechanisms get reversed. The entire institutional arrangement including judiciary to regulate power particularly the coercive completely break down. In the absence of ability to regulate, the civil administration starts agreeing with the arbitrary exercise of power under one pretext or the other. This also leads not what Riggs described 'overlapping of functions' but invasion of 'functional jurisdiction' of different institutions. This may include forest department, hospitals, colleges and universities, courts, media, trade unions, electoral processes and so on.

The central concern of entire administrative theory has been to see that behaviour of every member of the organisation is structured and institutionalised. All the organisational principles have their origins in this central concern. The 'relative autonomy' and arbitrary power logically lead to de-institutionalisation of behaviour. This happens as a result of the fact that the men at the cutting edge who are linked to the top through a chain of command can no more be held accountable to the consequences of their actions. The logic of the situation is that the arbitrary power percolates down the line and it is the man on the spot to whom this 'behavioural space' is conceded. Once such 'space' are admitted, the role of the higher levels of command change from 'command' to that of providing protective umbrella to the persons involved even in the most unlawful actions. In fact, it is this phenomenon that leads to the breakdown of all the accepted principles of organisation.

V

The above narration is only illustrative and not exhaustive. The significance of the narration lies in its potential for different conceptualisation of administrative phenomenon. A large part of the administrative theory including that of development administration is grounded in equilibrium centric paradigm. There has been some discussion on the role of development administration in causing change or handling change but change that is gradual, if not orderly. There is a wide gap in the corpus of knowledge as far as the explosive relation between the administrative system and the transformative movements is concerned. This can be a frontier area for enquiry in new public administration.

2

MOVEMENTS FOR EMPOWERMENT OF MINORITIES, WOMEN, SCHEDULED CASTES AND SCHEDULED TRIBES

Alice Vidya Sagar

Introduction

An empowerment movement could operationally be defined as a collective and organised effort sustained over a period of time, on behalf of low status groups for enhanced share in power in the public domain – social, cultural, political or economic. The empowerment movements are essentially those which address themselves to restoration of power balance that is lost due to historical contingencies or uneven development of different strata of society. They are apparently aimed at the enfranchisement of the disenfranchised, against the odds created, posed or abetted by the vested interests that stand to gain from such odds. Their thrust is the upward mobility of the status of the low status groups of subalterns.

There have been a plethora of movements for empowerment of subalterns throughout the course of history. These movements had their genesis and demise, ebbs and tides, shifting foci and loci, changing leadership and membership patterns through centuries. They are exogenous or endogenous in terms of their outside or inside inspiration respectively or in terms of central actors leading them. The religion, the state, civil society, citizen fora, community organisations had varying roles in promoting as well as arresting their progress and in changing their thrust and direction. The forms and contents of these movements have assumed and also been changing.

Civil rights movements, suffragette movements, feminist movements, freedom movements are some of the major empowerment movements that have been found across the world. The empowerment movements are different from country to country and within the country, from one historical era to another. Therefore, any meaningful discussion about them is possible only when they are properly contextualised.

India being a country of exceptional diversity and extreme inequalities of various kinds—social, political, economic and culturalù it has been the home for many of the empowerment movements throughout its chequered history. Among those various movements, those meant for empowerment of minorities, women, scheduled tribes are perhaps the most substantive as well as visible in contemporary India. These movements together make or mar the destinies of these various social groups and they have important implications for Indian economy, society and polity.

Empowerment Movements

Although different empowerment movements have commonalties in terms of the vulnerability of their members in their action instruments and in certain other matters, they have specificities too of their own. It is useful to discuss them here somewhat synoptically at least.

Subaltern movements have generally taken six different forms to empower their clientele. They are proselytisation (or religious conversions), education, agitation's for rights protection, lobbying for concessions and favours from the State, community organisations and class struggles, Christinisation, Islamisation, Neo-Budhistic conversions have been the dominant modes of proselytisation in modern times At times these conversions are accompanied by reconversions into the mainstream Hindu fold through "Shuddhi" process. These conversions and reconversions, which were particularly marked in the case of dalits and other lowly placed social groups, have avoided the neo-convertee, new identities and entitlements in the socio-cultural as well as politico-economic relations. It is not far from truth to assert that these conversions have generally afforded spaces for empowerment of subalterns through occupational mobility, economic development, educational equipment and cultural advancement. However, they have also resulted in weakening of the already tenuous solidarity among the weaker sections quite apart from precipitating bloody communal clashes in their wake. It is not without substance that some people claim that some of the denominational organisations have rendered greater yeomen service to the dalits than what the State could do for their redemption.

Several Community organisations, voluntary agencies, charitable trusts and religious bodies have made numerous attempts at education—both formal and informal—so as to raise the consciousness and cognitive levels of the depressed groups.

Education, quite apart from its generally liberating influence had given the neo-educated classes wherewithal to perceive and checkmate affronts to their rights and - entitlements. Education has also helped them to graduate themselves into decision-making centres.

They have also helped spur numerous agitations for rights assertions and empowerment as manifested in the form of temple entry movements of dalits, land struggles of tribals and other weaker sections, wage struggles and other forms of agrarian struggles. There has also been an accentuation of demand for greater power sharing through reservations related benefits on the State, political parties and other power ensembles. These attempts were met with varying degrees of success.

Community organisations refer to organisations and associations such as those based on caste, community or on alliance of castes etc. These organisations, sometimes negatively characterised as communal organisations, have mobilised their members on narrow lines for defensive or offensive purposes and for progressive and regressive causes. There has been upswing of such organisations in the recent times mainly with an eye on electoral advantages and they are sometimes promoted with ulterior motives. One major upshot of these mobilisations has been the increasing visibility of the subalterns in the political arena.

Class struggles are ideologically oriented and Left inspired and they have encompassed a wide spectrum of subalterns. These struggles have generally assumed the form of political parties and have sought structural changes in the economy. The struggles launched by the Left and Ultra-Left outfits have generally shown concern for all subalterns that have particularly articulated the needs of the poor and have-nots. They have focussed on economic issues following their Marxian premise of economic determinism. However, they have laterly been realising the counter-productiveness of their exclusive reliance on class basis and neglect of cultural basis such as caste, gender communistic discrimination. Their impact on empowerment of subalterns have been very marked but the impact has been localised and restricted to areas such as Kerala, West Bengal, Tripura and to certain pockets of Andhra Pradesh and Bihar. The class struggles spearheaded by the Leftist political parties and formations have initially been very radical and had been largely anti-state and anti-establishment. As such, the subalterns who were drawn to them had to bear the brunt of oppressive State action. In the later period, however, the bulk of the Indian Left had taken to parliamentary path resulting in the stateisation of class struggles. The extreme Left is still in the militant path but it is hopelessly fragmented to be of much consequence to therstale of empowerment of the have-nots. However, it still holds a radical alternative to the empowerment of subalterns and the sniffing of the fire kindled by it, is proving too daunting a job for the State to do. Closely related to the Leftist political formations are the various human rights groups such as the PUCL, PUDR, APCLC etc., which are exposing serious human rights violations by the State—in instances no one else would dare to question or confront it. Although these human rights groups are not able to prevent human rights abuses, their very presence has made it difficult for the State to conceal such abuses if not altogether avoid committing them.

Feature of Empowerment Movements

Now we come to the distinctive features of the four kinds of empowerment movements under reference :

(i) The Minority movements while asserting the distinctive identities of the minorities have tended to work for preservation of such identities and thus become conservative in their orientation. They have been progressive to the extent that they have been working for the material advancement of minorities. There are three different kinds of minorities in India and they are religious minorities, the linguistic minorities and the cultural minorities. These three major kinds of minorities are largely exclusive of each other and hence there has not been much common ground. The issues so far articulated by them comprise of organised resistance against attacks on minorities, preservation of their distinctive cultural attributes, reservation benefits, check-mating interference in Muslim Personal Law, sub-regionalism, official language questions, protection of person and property of minorities etc The minority movement has also resulted in party building as in the case of Indian Union Muslim League, [Jamaat-e- Islam-e-Hind, Akali Dal and have succeeded in holding the reins of power exclusively or as coalition partners as in Kerala and Punjab. Certain minority religious groups have taken to fundamentalist stances and have resorted to convert actions and to gain extra territorial support. Such groups have come to be the suspect in the eyes of the State and general population and have invited general antipathy towards minorities.

(ii) The women's movements or the feminist movements focussing on gender discrimination as their counterpoint have sought to empower women by fighting against gender specific debilities imposed up on them by custom, convention, state or civil society. They have questioned the bases of patriarchy, fought against the abuse of and violence against women, and have sought share in power. They have supported or even spearheaded temperance movement as poignantly demonstrated as in the case of the anti-barrack movement waged by women in AP, couple of years ago. The women's movement in India suffers form a number of limitations. Firstly, it is highly fragmented as evident form an absence of a pan-Indian women's movement. Secondly, it is largely confined to urban areas and has generally focussed its attention on small section of women population, such as the urban or middle class women. Thirdly, the movement did not result in founding the feminist parties as in the West.

(iii) The scheduled caste movement, also referred to sometimes as the Harijan movement or Dalit movement, fought against caste—bounded discrimination, against untouchability, for the exercise of civil rights and for securing an effective enforcement of reservation related concessions accorded by the State in the fields of political representation, public employment and higher education. The scheduled caste movement had both exogenous and endogenous inspiration in terms of its leadership base. The movement has sometimes assumed a distinct political form as exemplified on the founding of political formations like the Scheduled Castes Federation, the Republican Party and the Dalit Panthers. The influence of these political formations was short-lived and was confined to the western and northern parts of the country. The SC Movement has been highly fragmented but for a brief period when Dr Ambedkar was on the scene. The articulations of the SC movement have been largely urban and middle class oriented, it could not touch the core problems of the dalits like landlessness, poverty and deprivation in a major way.

(iv) The scheduled tribe movement, also referred to as Adivasi or Girijan movement, has been the most virulent of the different empowerment movements. The movements' basic concern has been the alienation of tribals from their land and livelihood due to the onslaught of narrowly conceived development policies. The tribal movement has assumed different forms like tribal fronts in the North-East, the Jharkhand Movement for separate homeland far Tribals and the Marxist Leninist movements in different parts of the country These various movements notwithstanding, there has been a progressive detereoration in the status of tribals leading to their unabated movement except in the North-East. The tribal movements, like most other subaltern empowerment movements have been largely fragmented. Tribal India could not so far produce leadership of the .stature of Ambedkar or even Jagjivan Ram, both of whom had a definite All-India following among the SCs.

Approaches of Study

The empowerment movements could be studied or approached from various standpoints and disciplinary perspectives. They could be approached from a historical perspective focussing on their genesis, growth and decline, their shifting foci and loci and their achievements and failures. They could be studied from the sociological perspective focussing on the social basis of their leadership and membership, their impact on social structure and dynamics, their issue bases and their articulations on issues, from an anthropological standpoint they could be studied with reference to their cultural impingements. From the perspective of economic science, their command over resources, sources of finance,, their impact on occupational and economic mobility, their effect on production relation could be analysed Viewed from a politico-administrative angle, their organisational forms, their political leanings, leadership patterns, their alliances and counter alliances, their nexus with parties and political formations, their ideological bases and their linkages with the State and the nature of such linkages could be brought under focus.

The above-stated approaches may not and need not be taken in isolation of each other. Ideally the empowerment movements need to be studied from a multi-disciplinary pespective wherein the movement's social roots, economic bases, cultural modes, organisational forms and political manifestations are all brought under focus all at once. However, depending on the emphasis laid on one or the other among the perspectives, the movements could be categorised and fixed into a particular mould, at the risk of over simplification notwithstanding.

In the light of the above discussion, the following themes may be identified for studies. This list is by no means exhaustive, it is only illustrative.

1. History of empowerment movements in general and the empowerment movements of the identified groups in particular.
2. The State and Employment Movements of Minorities / Women / SCs / STs.
3. Sub-Regional Movements.
4. Dalit/Harijan Movement(s).
5. Temple Entry Movement.
6. Civil Rights Movements.
7. Tribal/Adivasi/Girijan Movements.

8. Women's/Feminist Movement.
9. Social bases of Empowerment Movements.
10. Proselytisation and Anti-proselytisation Movements.
11. Regional Dimensions of Movements (eg. Dalit Movement in South/North/Western Central India).
12. Media and Empowerment Movements.
13. Literature and Empowerment Movements.
14. Human Rights Commission and Human Rights Groups.
15. Movement Leadership and Profiles of Leaders.
16. Minority or Subaltern Parties and their Contributions to Empowerment.
17. Anti-Dowry Movement.
18. The Left and the Empowerment of Subalterns.
19. Ideology of Empowerment.
20. Theoretical Perspectives on Empowerments.

Having dealt with the thematic background, and broader issues, I sincerely hope that the studies would focus on the Listed objectives of the conference and find solutions to maintain a people-friendly administration, which would respond favorably and regularly to the problems of the different sections of the people in India.

3

PERSPECTIVE OF CIVIL LIBERTIES : PERCEPTION

S. Sheshaiah and Gunti Ravi

The emergence of human rights movement entailed the historic facts like persisting economic imbalances, exploitation, repression and the ruling class tendencies. Human rights and the concept of enjoying those rights have got civil, economic, socio- cultural aspects of a particular citizen as its constituent parts. Oppressed sections all over the world have secured the civil and political rights by waging relentless struggles against the feudal and capitalist societies.

Even the history of evolution of society is clearly indicating the fact pertaining to the attainment of various kinds of basic changes in the system with the aid of strong political movements and armed revolutionary struggles. The political movements undertaken for the purpose of attaining social change are supported by human rights movements in their respective regions. People would fight for securing the civil and political rights during the course of their political struggles aimed at achieving social changes.

The Human rights movement or even the civil liberties movement would not remain in independent struggle form, but it would extend solidarity to the political and other kinds of democratic movements that are in vogue. It is this kind of strategy that would enable the movements to succeed. One has to view the civil rights and democratic rights movement in that angle only.

The capitalist ruling class has sensitised the masses about the availment of Liberty, Equality and Solidarity and the Rights Concept in a bid to counter the feudal classes during the initial stages of emergence of Human Rights Concept. Democratic rights in particular spread into the societies subsequent to their emergence from the bourgeois democratic revolutions apparently helping the capitalist societies to take firm roots. The awareness process during the later stages has instilled in the masses the confidence of being equal, irrespective of caste, creed and religion. However, the suppressed class in the capitalist countries continued its struggles seeking democratic rights in the later stages. It lasted for decades. Inequality among the citizens persisted till the beginning of the 20th century in several capitalist countries wherein working class, women and the underprivileged were subjected to harassment.

The capitalist society which brought about the theory of equality is merely translating that theory in the political arena and that too within the framework of the State and its organs. It creates hurdles in the path of underprivileged sections when they seek equality in the socio-economic fields. The capitalist class which enjoys supremacy over productive forces relies mainly on the exploitation imposed on the working class. It is owing to this reason the neobourgeois constitution opposed the provision of socio economic rights to the commoners. The rights during the course of realisation would become posers to the bourgeois classes and their monopoly tendencies. The human rights movement under these circumstances should lend a helping hand to the political movements that are emerging for the fulfillment of rights to everybody.

When we come to the point of socio-economic rights, the capitalist countries on the global front never recognised the need of providing the liberties to the masses till the fall of socialist camp subsequent to the Second World War. The Proletariat in the capitalist countries took right to work, minimum wages, rights for equality, rights for education and medical facilities, social security on the top priority of their agenda during the course of their fight against the ruling forces. This was also taken up after the socialist block consisting of Russia, China and Eastern European countries recognised the socio-economic rights as fundamental rights subsequent to their attainment of revolution in their respective countries. Though the capitalist countries never offer any guaranteed legality to the expedition of these rights, they were compelled to implement them atleast partially. Whenever the capitalist countries experience a threat to their existence, the proletariat rights were subjected to harassment. Ruling class in those countries at once exposed their real nature and resorted to fascist rule by unleashing a suppressing hand, This was evidenced after the Second World War period. On a number of occasions, the Fascist ruling classes in America and other countries tried to make an invasion into the backward nations and they even made bids to indulge in unnecessary interference in the internal matters of those nations, Even they tried to pose threat to the sovereignty of these nations by unleashing armed attacks .The invasion of Market forces from the 70's in the name of globalisation has also entailed the emergence of the civil rights movements in the needy zones. The tactics of imperialists on the backward nations are also helping the movements of civil right organisations to bolster their activity against the exploitation, oppression and antidemocratic activities.

Semi-colonial and semi-feudal countries like India are in dire need of civil right movements. Even the bourgeois democracy is not tangible in India. A major chunk of population in the country is spending a poor and miserable life. They are not enjoying the fundamental rights guaranteed by the Constitution. Minimum Wages Act, Equal work-Equal pay Act, Act promulgated to eradicate untouchability, and child labour Act, rights pertaining to organising meetings, formulating associations, waging protests have become nominal in the country. For instance, the minimum wages act formulated for the uplift of working class has not been implemented anywhere in the country in its true spirit. When the working class tried to realise unity among themselves demanding the fulfillment of these rights, the government has created many hurdles and the guaranteed fundamental rights in the Constitution are going useless. In some cases, working class and factory workers including the agricultural laborers were subjected to harassment for organising the workers onto a platform. They were sacked and harassed for their participation in agitation against the establishment and even the last resort of banning strikes was also imposed. The violation of fundamental rights in the country and even the suspension of certain fundamental rights have become quite common. Our Constitution in itself is fleeced with undemocratic concepts. Patriarchy and male chauvinism and right to decision-making are some of the things that are incorporated in the Constitution. The State is protecting the interests of those for exploitation by resorting to the preservation of property right. It is shielding the landlords, capitalists, black marketers and the corrupt. Similarly, people are deprived of the fundamental rights guaranteed by the Constitution, whenever the people's movements erupt. The Constitution grabs the so-called democratic rights in the name of maintenance of law and order and other so-called democratic norms.

The ruling class resorts to violation of 'framed' rights by branding the champions of civil rights as the violators. It imposes certain acts vested with special powers on the people such as TADA, PD Act, MISA, NSA, Armed Forces Special Power Act, Disturbed Area Act, Act pertaining to death sentence illegally. Similarly, the legality of impositions is extended even to the banning of political parties, frontal units, peoples activists and peoples literature. This is the nature of Indian democracy.

Under these circumstances, the civil rights movement should chalk out its plan of action. The civil rights movement in itself is not a class struggle and the civil rights organisations would not lead the movements involving class struggles. However, the movements undertaken with an aim to bring about a change in the society are supported by the civil rights activists. The civil rights groups extend solidarity to the democratic organisations during the course of democratisation of class struggles.

These groups basically concentrate on exposing the deeds that are perpetrated by the State in the form of repression and other suppressive measures. The civil rights groups pay much attention to condemn the State violence during the course of their activity and it is the main responsibility of civil rights movement. If this thing is not adopted, the civil rights activity would not be strengthened in the needy zones and the nefarious designs of State and its organs are not exposed clearly. It is this aspect that provides civil rights movement to formulate its duties and responsibilities.

STATE - LAW - SOCIETY

State and law are the two social aspects that have come into being during the process of historical development. The bourgeois democratic theory opines that the State was established 'for the people, by the people and of the people', Similarly, the judiciary is also termed as a system evolved to settle the issues that are confronted by the people. Both these organs create an impression that they work for the welfare of the people. Similarly, people thought that these systems would be useful to them in resolving their issues and problems.

Indian Constitution is taking the people for granted that the citizens are equal and they can enjoy the rights and liberties guaranteed by the Constitution, The Constitutional Law of India, 1935 is itself an undemocratic document. This document guarantees the citizens civil and political rights and that too within a specified framework. The Constitution then did not attest recognition of right to work, free education, health facilities, shelter and other socio-economic aspects. They were incorporated in the Directive Principles. The civil rights concept is not guaranteeing rights to minorities and right of self-determination to nationalities. Even the Constitution and the guaranteed rights are in the clutches of imperialist forces to enjoy and violate according to their whims and fancies.

Freedom and property rights in the present system are determined with respect to the social status of the individuals, but not as guaranteed in the Constitution and law of the land.

Freedom and independence are at the disposal of a citizen as long as the property right assumes social nature without succumbing to personal pressures. The state prefers to protect the vested interests of property related issues of certain productive forces in a system where exploitation and oppression rule the roost.

The law of the land is providing enough opportunity to the ruling classes to enjoy and continue their dominance on the society. In the process, it enables the ruling classes to impinge the guaranteed rights. Law defines all the rights including the property right incorporated in the Constitution. It determines the public relations. State makes use of law as an instrument to direct and decide the relations pertaining to production.

State and law of the land are imposing the ruling class ideology on the oppressed sections with an ulterior motive. The state is the ultimate weapon utilised by the ruling classes to expand their exploitation methods. Criminal law appends universality to oppression, exploitation and other ruling class tendencies. However, the nature of state and criminal law assumes several changes with the emergence of movements and struggles. Similarly, the oppressive tendencies and intensity of oppression would depend upon the intensity of movements and on the awareness of masses.

State in India is providing enough opportunities to protect the ruling class tendencies like dominant nature in the society exploitation and repressive measures. It is in a way promoting the ruling class interests by extending a helping hand to the patriarchal, casteist and property based system. Similarly, it is encouraging the systematic violence and repression adopted by the ruling forces. Under these circumstances, the civil liberties movement should guide the masses to awake. These organisations should provide the needed animation to the masses about the relationship between state and society besides sensitising them, about the nature of socio-productional relations. The civil liberties organisations are bestowed with the responsibility of fighting for the securing of rights to the oppressed sections as well as for the aid of Dalit sections like women in the patriarchial societies.

Revolt on a system is regarded a crime according to the law of the land. It defines the activities of the democratic organisations in the similar context without taking the aims and objectives of movements into consideration. The law of the land never recognises the solidarity movements enjoying and simply identifies movements as problems pertaining to socio-political matters. In this way, criminal law depoliticises the struggle and individualises the dispute and thereby disorganises the movement.

Masses and oppressed sections are compelled to take to struggle path protesting against inequalities, dominant nature, exploitation and insecure nature that are inflicted on them under the influence of capitalism. They become a part of movements to settle the issues that are confronted by them. In a bid to counter the awareness, State imposes repression and unleashes a reign of terror on movements. The Constitutional network imposes stringent measures on the activists by violating all kinds of rights like freedom of expression, right to conduct meetings and other forms of civil rights that are guaranteed to the masses. Masses require civil and political rights to protect the liberties like right to live, right to take to struggle in the course of living in the society. The right to take to struggles would have an immense impact in the societies where the issues are not settled with out any protest.

Social and personal rights differ with each other in a bourgeois society. This difference would emerge from the facts like economic imbalances and dominant characteristics. For instance, the law of the land terms the activities undertaken by the working class as crimes when the farm laborers occupy the lands of landlord sections. During the process, the law brands the working class as criminals. Similarly, the right to take to agitations though agreed to by the law has not been recognised as fundamental right. When the agitation takes the militant form and threatens the interests of the managements and poses a threat to their lives, agitation would become a crime according to law. However, the civil liberties movement should give top priority to the group rights at the expense of personal rights.

State requires a propaganda where it tries to focus itself as an independent set-up in order to gain profits through invested capitals and through capitalist-product relations. Power in the state is vested on the forces whose supremacy remains on the productive forces. This aspect is not exposed and it would remain a part of many complicated issues. The state would be having independent stature in order to expose its nature of management—working class equality before the law. However, the state ultimately supports the ruling class whenever the ruling and ruled classes differ on issues.

The inequalities and other imbalances in the Indian system are enabling the democratic revolutionary movements and other forms of democratic movements to take roots in the society. Nationality movements on the demand of self-determination, women struggles in protest against the patriarchal setup and male chauvinist society, dalit movements exposing the exploitation of upper caste dominated casteist society and movements highlighting environment importance are some of the democratic forms that are recognised as the primary

efforts to the democratic movements by civil rights movement. The state unleashes a reign of terror by spreading its Fascist tentacles whenever it befools the mass struggles posing threat to its existence. Black and draconian laws are imposed on the public by violating the norms of existing liberties. Armed repression is imposed upon the movements with an iron hand. While the above facts are highlighting the reality, the Indian setup is grossly enabling the ruling class and dominant sections to enjoy the powers and laws that are guaranteed in the Indian constitution.

The black and draconian laws are shielding the black marketers and capitalist scamsters in the existing setup. They are failing utterly in curbing the spurt in black marketers, capitalist scamsters and feudal forces and their private armies. Even the anti-national forces and the upper class lobbies were offered olive branches by the existing setup. Apart from this, the state is extending maximum support to these forces.

On the other hand, the feudal imperialist culture existing in the present society is inflicting unemployment, insecurity, starvation and other ill effects on the society. It is in a way helping the crime graph rise to alarming proportions. These are supported and carried out by the capitalist feudal forces whose dominance is persistently increasing in the present system. Under these circumstances, death sentence has become a weapon in the armory of ruling forces to impose upon the democratic forces and common criminals including the weak forces, of course 'legally'. This sentence is being imposed deliberately on the democratic forces who are waging relentless struggles against exploitation and other forms of oppression. These impositions are in a way painting the living right of commoners black.

The liberal bourgeoisie in the civil liberties movement is of the opinion that the constitutional system like courts, laws, police, military and the official machinery can be utilised for attaining the democratic rights to the commoner. It is feeling that the Indian state was neutral in its nature and it has got the capacity of sufficing the commoners' interests. These elements having certain wrong notions over the bourgeoisic democracy, feel that the civil and human rights would be guaranteed to the masses more in a capitalist setup than in the socialist setup.

They contradict the versions of others and maintain freedom to individual, including civil liberties were a distant dream in the socialist setup. Parliamentary set up, law and the written constitution are regarded the basic ingredients of democracy by these forces. They resort to a malicious propaganda, saying the proletariat in Russia, China and Eastern Europe has let down the democratic rights subsequent to the emergence of working class rule. Similarly, the liberal bourgeoisie resort to a propaganda that the Communists perpetrate state violence and dictatorship in their countries. They come to these wrong conclusions by guaging the democracy in an abstract nature and by not considering the chronological changes subsequent to the attainment of proletariat revolutions.

Democracy in bourgeoisie setup is enjoyed mainly by the exploiting classes. It never extends any sort of help to the masses. The proletariat and the oppressed can protect their democratic rights only by way of waging struggles against the feudal, capitalist and other exploiting classes. This sort of opinion must be created among tho majority masses wherein they would be sensitised about the attainment of democracy through the occupation of properties of exploiting classes.

Human rights movements are essential in people's republics and socialist nations. It is essential since the economic inequalities and exploitation of previous society exist to some extent in these nations and similarly the cultural exploitation methods that persist with the society can be wiped out not only with the aid of political movements but also with human rights movements.

People's participation and their role in the contemplation of policies and product-oriented strategies are not evident in a capitalist setup. People enjoy the status of a complete citizen only in the voting right. However, some semi feudal and semi colonial states are even grabbing this right by resorting to booth capturing and rigging. People in these nations never enjoyed socio-economic rights. Here the liberal bourgeois intellingentia should note that the socialist nations like Russia, China and eastern European countries during the proletariat rule have provided individual freedom alongwith right to work, socio- economic rights besides enjoying the right to enjoy the power and participation in power. These rights were denied only when the revisionist forces made an influx into the ruling place. Then social fascism replaced it by ruling the roost. People made a revolt in the eighties against this kind of social fascism. The liberal bourgeois should take note of the point that revolt is a historical fact whenever civil rights are denied to the majority class.

Imperialist countries are deliberately differentiating the human rights from history and class factors. This policy would not exceed the limits of productive forces' individuality and individual freedom. Freedom and independence are restricted to laws and books by these units. They never agree the fact that the economic and various kinds of exploitations are the violation of human rights. Owing to this, they are focusing the State violence and the mass retaliations and resurgence in the same frame. This rigid opinion of human rights activists is helping the ruling class. The same opinion is utilised by the imperialist forces and their monetary units. The human rights movements in our country is unfortunately influenced by the international human rights organisations like Amnesty International. In the long run, this aspect is showing an adverse impact on the movement and in practice it is serving the interests of the exploiting ruling sections. A strong civil liberties movement can be constructed only when the problems of people and their rights are thoroughly studied and that too by considering the fact of class culture and divisive nature of the exploiting society.

Consideration of rights of exploiting sections and the rights of masses staging revolts in a single line can become a vague comparison, though the opinions like people's unity and the need to support their rights by civil liberties movement can be one of the factors. The civil liberties movement condemns the violation and denial of mass rights vehemently. It denounces the oppressive techniques of ruling class and exposes the nature of the state as and when it directly or indirectly supports such tendencies. Civil liberties movement considers resurgence against state violence and revolt against suppressions as the constituents of democratic rights. It extends similar kind of support to the unified activities of mass organisations and political parties who strive towards the attainment of democratic revolution.

The movement would not be having any interest to condemn the counter violence acts that are carried out by mass organisations. There won't be any need to condemn such acts. Since civil liberties movement is a constituent part of Indian democratic movements, it extends support to counter violent acts. If the movement of civil liberties differs from this kind of strategies, it would delink itself with the people and democratic movements. We have to understand the real nature of Indian state. Otherwise, we would fail utterly in understanding the suppression and exploitation on the civil and democratic rights. The civil liberties movement should animate the masses by carrying out an awareness drive during the course of activity. It should sensitize the people about the nature of mass struggles without considering the incidents of violation of rights and attacks on democratic movements separately. The civil rights movement should expose the state repression and the suppression of rights openly. Similarly, it should condemn the oppressive tendencies of the state unleashed on nationality struggles and should expose the dictatorial attitudes of state thoroughly. It should educate the masses about self determination right of nationalities.

Civil liberties movement would not be having any responsibility to judge the pros and cons of strategies and constructive methods of mass struggles openly. These 'judgements' would in a way harm the interests of mass struggles and they would indirectly help the state to suppress the movements.

The civil liberties movement should analyse the socio-economic factors behind certain mutinies where sections among the suppressed clans like Naga-Kuki, Adivasi Tripura-Bengali, Bodo-Santal, Hindu-Muslim and Hindu-Sikh are involved in them. They should expose the conspiracy of the state and ruling class behind these outbursts. It should also highlight the 'divide and rule' policy adopted by the exploited ruling classes and expose the real nature of them by how the majority masses were divided by those forces with a strategic approach for their vested interests. It should educate how the people in those sections were feeling insecured. On several occasions, the civil liberties organisations have to act as mediators between people and government, working class and managements. Under these circumstances, the organisation should stand beside the people in resolving the issues.

The civil liberties organisations should deliberate with the government in resolving the issues considering the larger interests of people and working class. The organisation should not resort to reach to any kind of agreement on the pretext that the issue be settled peacefully. The civil liberties mediators should not even compromise themselves on the pretext that the demands are bulky. When they feel the issue would not be settled in favour of the people, they should drop off mediation efforts.

It is inevitable that the civil rights activists and the leadership of civil right movement face the repression during the course of a considerable spurt in mass movements. The government would target the civil rights activists in the wake of their involvement with the people's struggles. The exposure of state's real nature and the condemnation of state violence besides the extension of support to the democratic rights movements are some of the reasons that would make the civil liberty movements as the enemies of state. The state in turn would launch a malicious propaganda that the activists were having a nexus with clandestine outfits and foreign elements. It tries to alienate the activists from the society and makes efforts to attack them. Similarly, the state would resort to some more techniques to weaken the spirit of civil liberties activists by creating terror among the cadre and by resorting to kidnaps, killings and by arresting the key cadres. The state would even perpetrate to terrorising acts and demoralises the cadre with its actions. The civil liberties movement should prepare itself psychologically to attain its goal.

If the civil liberties movement has to bolster itself as struggle form, it should take roots and strengthen itself from the grass roots of the society. Similarly, the district and town bodies be strengthened accordingly. We cannot carry forward the movement by relying on certain people. When those people degenerate, the movement would put to heavy losses, initially the movement can rely on the guidance of particular individuals but during the process of strengthening it, the organisation should contemplate the decision-making bodies unitedly. Otherwise, the movement would not attain the desired goal. The civil liberties movement should chalk out a programme wherein the democratic values like constructive system be promoted.

Otherwise, the people would not believe the organisation as a fore runner of the awakening movements.

The need of civil liberties movement would become essential with the emergence of class struggles at various levels. These movements should expose the real nature of state's oppressive tendencies thoroughly. They should take up various forms of struggles like mobilising the support of commoners in the form of accumulation of opinions and by taking up struggles and demonstrations. They should openly take up demonstrations and conduct meetings. Similarly, they should support the struggles undertaken by sections where the feudal's atrocities on farm sector, capitalists' oppressive tendencies on working class, Imperialist suppressive acts, upper caste tendencies, atrocities on women, oppression of ruling and fascist forces on minorities, nationalities and other oppressive tendencies. Through that form the civil liberties movement would discharge its responsibilities thoroughly.

4

HUMAN RIGHTS MOVEMENTS – CIVIL LIBERTIES

P. Veeraiah

India has parliamentary type of government in which the citizens have been given certain duties, responsibilities and also some fundamental rights, a salient feature of the Indian constitution. The demand for the incorporation of fundamental rights in Indian constitution may be traced back to 1920's. The Nehru Report (1928) recommended for the necessity of the incorporation of these rights in the future constitution. Later on, several demands were made by the Indian National Congress also. The fundamental rights as enjoyed by the Indian citizens now were incorporated in the constitution by the constituent assembly on the basis of recommendation of fundamental rights sub-committee headed by Sardar Patel. These rights aimed at the promotion of liberty, equality, fraternity and justice to the people and good conduct among them. Provision of social justice to the Scheduled castes, Scheduled tribes, weaker sections and minorities etc. are some of the important objectives of these rights. The features of fundamental rights to help in the development and growth of the personality of the individuals. They are enforced by a special machinery i.e. the Supreme Court of India and various High Courts in India. All Indian citizens enjoy these rights. Aliens also enjoy some of these rights. They are not absolute, may be restricted or suspended by the government depending upon the circumstances. They act as restraints upon the legislature, executive and judicial powers of the state. They apply not only to the state and also various agencies, but also to private individuals or organisations. They have been incorporated in the Constitution in Part III from articles 12 to 35. Dr. Ambedkar described them as the heart and soul of the constitution. These rights aim to inculcate the individual for his all-round development and also works as a check and prevent the misuse of power, authority by the concerned. Without rights, life will become miserable and the individuals are not sure about their lives, property, protection etc. Subsequently ,these rights lead to establish 'Human Rights Movement' around the world which are very essential for the safety and security of human beings. In general, human rights are those rights which are essential for the maintenance of human rights and worth. These rights are variedly called as natural rights, fundamental rights or bill of rights. It was first used by 'Roosevelt' in his message at the time of drafting the charter of United Nations at Sanfransisco.

The human rights though very old, got the impetus only after the adoption of the United Nations Charter in 1945 and the Universal Declaration of Human Rights in 1948. Over fifty international instruments (countries) have been adopted to protect Human Rights. These instruments together set common standards for all people and all nations. They set a comprehensive system and detailed procedure to look into country situations or categories of abuses that are occurring around the world. The rights and peace are indivisible and without the protection of human rights, there can be neither lasting security nor sustained economic and social development. The universal declaration of human rights recalls that the recognition of the inherent dignity and of the cruel and inalienable rights of all members of the human family in the foundation of the freedom, justice and peace in the world. Though there are impressive records of the United Nations, still violations are rampant every day, every hour in each and every religion and abuses are taking place.

A debate amongst philosophers and political thinkers for over centuries regarding the concept of the state and relationship between the ruler and the ruled. So called concept of the Divine right of the parliament or the more the doctrine of the fascists finding away of the individual in front of the omnipotent personalities of the state.

Autocratic rulers in the past had considered thenmselves as the fount of all rights and liberties. The will of the society was regulated by laws. The danger to rights and liberties if the individual became a cause of concern for the entire world and there is a need to the emergence of a new policy of thinking. Human rights are not new, these rights were recognised far back in the history in some of the Greek states who were familiar with modern concept of freedom of speech, equality before the law, equal respect of all. Most of the countries recognised the basic human rights. They were mentioned in the minorities that is after the First World War in the Paris peace treaties with Italy, Romania, Bulgaria, Hungary and Finland. A clause was added by which each state concerned undertook to take all measures necessary to secure to all persons under the jurisdiction without any difference in race, sex, language or religion and freedom of expression. But the covenant of the league of nations did not contain any provision regarding human rights. The Second World War changed man's thought in a manner never known before and after the recognition of the human rights.

The General Assembly of the United Nations on 10-12-1948 adopted universal declaration of Human Rights as a common standard of achievement of all the peoples for all the nations. Keeping in view of this, society shall keep this declaration constantly in mind and shall strive to promote respect for human rights. The United Nations Charter in Article 55 and 56 have provided to promote high standard of living, full employment with working conditions, solution of international economic, social, health and related problems and respect for and observance of human rights and fundamental freedom for all without any difference.

Dr. Martin Luther King Jr. said injustice any where is bound to lead to injustice every where. In the year 1966, the General Assembly adopted the covenant on civil and political rights, economic and political rights and covenant against all kinds of racial discriminations. But the difficulty lies not in recognising the human rights but in trying to enforce them. Now what is needed to evolve a system of adjudication on the International patterns, The Europeans convention on Human rights provides a machinery since 1953 and aims at guaranteeing certain fundamental rights and freedoms. They have European commissions of Human Rights, European Court of Human Rights, and Committee of Ministers of the Council of Europe.

In India the framers of the constitution were inspired by the universal declaration and they thought there is a need for affirming them and suitably protecting them.

This was evidenced in the preamble of the constitution (fundamental rights). Besides these the Directive Principles of State Policy are to act as guides for the state towards the establishment of a Just society, Article 13, 14, 15, 16, 19, 20(1), 20(2), 20(3), 23 and 24 were provided to safeguard the individual rights and freedom. In addition to several laws of a reformative character prohibit debt bondage, dowries, immoral traffic in women, validate -intercaste marriages and secure maternity benefits, protection of children, upliftment of the backward classes, Employees State Insurance Act, Minimum Wages Act, protection of civil rights etc. have been enforced. Though women population occupies more than half of the race are subjected to deprivation and discrimination in every walk of life, elimination of all forms of discrimination against women in the recent conventions. The 1974 report of the commission on the status of women also mentioned about discrimination against women. Deprived on the basis of sex, caste, colour, creed and national reasons, violence against women within their houses is a brutal fact. Discrimination against women in service sector is terribly pronounced, the harassment faced by women at work place is yet another problem of Human Rights.

The administrative machinery at the Central level and state level are under the chairmanship of Supreme Court Judge and High Court Judge with other members recommended and nominated by the President and Governors. Powers of the Human Rights commission are to investigate negligence of Human Rights. It may enquire and demand evidence etc, may investigate enquiry compliance. The commission may recommend the concerned governments to see the matter and to prevent and grant funeral support to the victims, go against the armed forces also. After due process, to initiate such action for violaltion of Human Rights, The concerned governments must implement with in three months the recommendations made by such commission. The commissions are established and functioning in the states of Assam, Madhya Pradesh, Uttar Pradesh, Haryana, Jammu and Kashmir, Punjab and Andhra Pradesh.

Major achievements of the Human Rights Commission are review of facts, visited terrorists places in Punjab and Andhra Pradesh, visited number of jails and sugggested ways and means to be followed towards the jail inmates. Conducted enquiries about custodian deaths, rapes, tortures etc. So far the commissions received complaints numbering forty thousand. The commission immediatley find out the facts and figures and ask the concerned governments to implement the same without any delay. It also recommends not only for and about Human Rights but also eradication of illiteracy, abolition of child labour, improving conditions of jails etc.

We may come to the conclusion that though there are a number of laws, rules and regulations to protect the human rights, the laws and acts alone would not stop the harassment, ill treatment, inhuman behaviour etc. until there is a change in the human behaviour. Then and then only we can expect a change in the society with good hope.

5

ENVIRONMENTAL MOVEMENTS : IMPLICATIONS FOR PUBLIC ADMINISTRATION

R.K. Sapru

INTRODUCTION

Environmental problems have been persisting at local, regional and international levels. Today, environmental pollution is by far the most serious and irrecoverable problem. Consequently, the deterioration of the quality of environment has become the subject of discussion and intensive research in both developed and developing nations. Halting and reversing ecological degradation, which has now assumed dangerous proportions, has been identified as a major priority in a growing volume of national and international studies and reports. No developments which does not find a solution to the cause of environmental impoverishment is worthy of its name.

Research findings in environmental monitoring and biological sciences, combined with harsh experiences in international economic development, have made the world community realise that its own health and well-being and the fate of future generations depend on—action to avert environmental catastrophe. This new understanding has helped to bring into sharper focus the interrelatedness of environment and development. It emphasises the importance of ensuring a healthy relationship between man and his environment on which his survival depends.

Industrial, agricultural, and alike activities and deforestation on a massive scale without environmental consideration can cause serious environmental impoverishment in turn impairing the quality of life of present and future generations. Environmental movements have been created, mobilised and organised from time to time to draw the attention of the local community, industrialists and public authorities about the complexity of issues causing environmental pollution . A brief survey of environmental problems facing India is portrayed here :

(i) India has a land mass of nearly 329 million hectares (2.4% of the total land area of the world) of which 175 million hectares are degraded mainly caused by water and wind erosion (141.3 m. hec).

(ii) Although the country has a great diverse forest vegetation, it is dwindling due to overgrazing, over-exploitation, encroachments, unsustainable practices, forest fire and indiscriminate siting of development projects in the forest areas. Presently, the recorded forest area is 76.52 million hectare which works out to 23.3 percent of the total geographical area and actual forest; cover is 63,3 million hectare, which constitutes only 19.3 per cent of the total land area, as against the National Forest Policy 1988 stipulation of a target of 33 percent. Even within this recorded area, only 36.7 million hectare, or only 11.2 percent of country's total land area, comprises dense forest.

(iii) The country has a rich repository of biological resources, and its bio-diversity contributes 8 per cent of the known global biological diversity. Yet over-exploitation and loss of habitat is leading to the extinction of various plants, animals and microbial species. According to estimates, over 1500 plant species are endangered and about 79 mammals, 44 birds, 15 reptiles, 3 ambphibians and several insects species are listed as endangered. Such a biological condition of the country is a serious threat to sustainable advances in biological productivity.

(iv) **Air Pollution :** High concentration of sulphur dioxide (SO) and suspended particulate matter (SPM) occurring in about 20 percent of the cities are caused by domestic use of coal or bio-mass fuel, growing industrialisation and increasing vehicular pollution. The toxic nature of air pollutants and their high concentrations in many industrialised regions are posing serious concerns both in terms of human health and damage to man-made structures and to country's ecology in general.

Water Pollution : Water pollution is by far the most serious in its implications for health and well-being of the people. A staggering 70 percent of the available water in India is polluted. The rising industrial and domestic wastes have resulted in heavy stress of pollution of water bodies such as: lakes, rivers, coastal areas and underground sources. A 1994 survey of ground water quality at 138 sampling locations in 22 industrialised zones indicated that water was unfit for drinking due to high bacteriological and heavy metal contamination.

More than half of the cities have no sewage. Access to safe drinking water, thus, remains an urgent need : 85 percent of the population in the urban areas and 79 percent in rural areas have access to safe drinking water. Urban Municipal wastes (MSW) is a heterogeneous mixture of paper, plastic, cloth, metal, glass, organic matter etc. generated from households, commercial establishments and markets.

Solid Waste and Coastal Pollution : Based on surveys carried out, the urban solid wastes generated in 1997 was estimated at 48 million tonnes. It is also estimated that 35-40 million tonnes of flyash is generated annually by the thermal power plants of which only 2-3 percent is currently being utilised.

In addition, in large quantities of industrial and hazardous wastes brought about by expansion of chemical based industry has compounded the wastes management problem with serious environmental health implications.

Further, an important impact of climate change and global warming may be the rise in sea level. The primary effect of sea level rise will increase coastal flooding, erosion, storm surges and wave activity.

MAJOR CAUSES OF ENVIRONMENTAL PROBLEMS

Environmental degradation is the consequence of interplay of social, economic and political factors. Population growth is itself a major source of environmental degradation when it exceeds the threshold limits of the support systems. Poverty too is both the cause and effect of environmental degradation.

Rapid growth of urban population and unplanned expansion of cities has resulted in deterioration of air and water quality, disposal of wastes, the proliferation of slums, all of which contribute to environmental impoverishment Intensive agriculture and irrigation, extensive use of pesticides contribute to land degradation and water pollution.

ENVIRONMENTAL MOVEMENTS

Environmental movements have been organised and launched in both developing and developed countries largely with the motive of creating awareness among the masses about the need of preserving and protecting the environmental resources.

1. Friends of the Earth International

Friends of the Earth International was founded in 1971 by national organisations from the USA, Great Britain, Sweden and France, and is known as one of the important international networks of environmental movements. It organises campaigns, distributes valuable information to its members all over the world, stimulates bilaterial cooperation and helps with fund-raising. Activists from all over the world not only discuss environmental problems, but also their strategies, different political and possibilities to cooperate internationally on a practical level.

The philosophy of FOE International can be found in the slogan "Think Globally, Act Locally". The members of FOE International from the first day, were convinced that the environmental problem was becoming more and more a threat to earth as a whole, and to the possibilities for humankind to survive on it.

At present the Friends of the Earth International (FOE International) is a network of 32 organisations in 32 countries (15 in Western Europe, 5 each in Latin America and Asia-Pacific, 2 each in North America, Africa and Australia / New Zealand and 1 in Eastern Europe.

The main decisions with FOEI are taken at the Annual General Meeting. Every member-organisation, of whatever size or financial contribution, has one vote. The Executive Committee consists of 7 members from three continents.

However, each national FOE-group stays autonomous. It is by no way bound to join FOE International activities. It can decide on its own arguments. At the moment FOE International has four international campaigns; on air pollution, on tropical rain forests, on nuclear issues, on marine issues and wetlands. In Europe, a fifth campaign to stop the destruction of environment in and around the Mediterranean has started.

Every campaign has its own structure. The Air Pollution Campaign is organised partly in cooperation with WISE (World Information Service on Energy) and FOE U.K., FOE Holland, Ireland, Poland, USA and Canada do another part of the job. The Tropical Rain Forest Campaign is organised by the regional networks, one coordinated by FOE U.K., one by Sahaliat Alam Malaysia (which means Friends of the Earth Malaysia) and the third one by the Rain forest Action Network in the USA. There is also cooperation from the World

Wildlife Fund. The Nuclear Campaign is coordinated by FOE, Ireland and FOE UK. The Mediterranean Campaign is coordinated by FOE Spain and Brussel. The Marine activity is coordinated by lobbying international bodies, member-governments and a Dutch organisation.

The International Secretariat in London publishes a bimonthly bulletin called FOE Link besides FOE Newspaper which is a bi-annual publication. FOE does not have a well elaborated, officially adopted solution for the environmental problems.

The environmental movements in the West not only attacked the carelessness of industrialists and politicians, as regards the future, but also developed alternatives, like "soft energy paths" plans for reducing waste by recycling and so on.

Now at the international level, most governments have adopted an environmental policy. International bodies, like the United Nations and the FOE try to coordinate environmental measures. Environmental organisations are accepted phenomena. They have been given a modest place in the social field of forces comparable with consumer's associations or sometimes even trade unions. But by far this is not enough. Firstly, part of the pollution and threats are being exported to the third world or the Eastern European countries. Secondly, the industrialised countries keep on consuming a gigantic part of the world's resources, not only their "own" part, but also minerals, soil, clean air, water and even labour of the third, world. About a quarter of the world's population, who live in these industrial societies, consume at least 75% of all resources.

But the fight for environment and a better future for humankind can only succeed if environmentalists cooperate internationally.

2. Cordillera People's Struggle for Self-Determination

The successful resistance of the people against the

attempted construction of the Chico River Dam in the Cordillera highlands of north Philippines is one of many landmarks in Cordillera's history where people asserted their right to self-determination. The people's opposition to the project also received support from human rights groups and environmentalists all over the world. Now there is a Cordillera People's Alliance (CPA) which has grown to 130 organisations with a membership of about 40,000. It continues to serve the communities by engaging in people-oriented socio-economic progammes and ecologically sound development projects.

3. The Greenham Common Movement

The Women's peace camp outside the barbed wire fence in the USA Greenham Common has been in existence now for 20 years during which time the women have camped, demonstrated, painted, talked and blockaded in an attempt to persuade as many people as will listen and think about the actuality of nuclear war. Under the Peace Camp in December 1983, fifty thousand women gathered to protest against the arrival of the first of missiles. Since the setting up of the Womens Peace Camp at Greenham Common, other women camps have been set up in New York where missile parts are made, in Pine Gap monitoring base in Australia and Holland. There are also mixed peace camps in England, Scotland, Germany, Belgium, Holland and Sicily.

4. Enron's Dabhol Power Plant and People Resistance

The US multinational giant, the Enron Development Corporation and the Maharastra government had to face resistance from the people of the Konkan region when the corporation set out to prospect the possibility of setting up a 2015 megawatt power project in a remote village Weldur. Although the project has successfully obtained all the necessary environmental clearances and going ahead, the way in which local people had organised themselves to oppose the project and the questions raised by them about the government's industrial policy are relevant in themselves. The residents of the Konkan belt feared that the pollutants emanating from the industries in the area will eventually have an adverse effect on their fruit crops. For the marginal farmers who have lost their land, the issue is one of survival. "What can we do with money without land? How will we fill our stomachs ?"

Villagers of the Konkan coast felt that they would be forced to become wage labourers and urban migrants. They refused to accept payment for their land which has already been acquired by the Maharashtra Industrial Development Corporation for Dabhol Power Company (DPC).

Besides, resistance from the local people, DPC had to face a number of court cases filed by groups questioning its environmental safeguards as well as the financial terms. The liquified natural gas (LNG) based thermal power plants are considered to be clean. One of the objections raised to the DPC is its potential to contribute to pollution when it will use distillate oil. Another environmental objection that has been raised is about the potential damage to local fishing resulting from the discharge of hot water into the sea.

Mr. Ashok Kadam of the Konkan Sangharsh Samiti argued that the issue is not the DPC but the other industries that are bound to follow and the combined effect of such industrialisation on the environment of the area. The apprehension that their lush and fertile country side will be rendered barren and polluted.

5. Sardar Sarovar Project and The Narmada Bachao Andolan

The Narmada Bachao Andolan (NBA) spearheaded by Ms. Medha Patkar is another environmental movement concerned with demand for stoppage of work on the Sardar Sarovar Project as the necessary steps to resettle the affected population in Madhya Pradesh had not been taken. Even more meaningful for the NBA was a report by the Sardar Sarovar Displaced Inquiry Committee which stated that only 2 percent of the 33014 families in MP who are in the submergence area of the SSP have been rehabilitated so far. " The problems that we saw", stated the report, "include people who have been displaced without cultivable land being available and who have been given unproductive land."

6. Shrimp Farms Controversy in Tamil Nadu

In Tamil Nadu there are strong protests from environmentalists and social activists demanding the closure of shrimp farms in the coastal areas of Tamil Nadu.

Environmentalists say that while the sweeping "blue revolution" in the State has ushered in economic prosperity to shrimp farm promoters in general and a few corporate giants in particular, it has wrought an ecological disaster, with the desertification of fertile lands in village abutting the shrimp farms. This according to them, poses a danger to the very livelihood of farm labour and fisherman in the coastal belt of Thanjavar and Nagapattinam-Quaid-E-Milleth (NQM) districts, considered the granary of the state.

They regret that despite a ban on the setting up of shrimp farms in cultivable lands, nearly 1,200 acres of fertile land have so far been taken over by shrimp farm promoters in Sirkazhi taluk of NQM district and in the Thanjavur coastal belt.

What is pathetic is that even those unwilling to fall in line find that they have no option but to sell their lands as the adjoining shrimp farms discharge untreated toxic effluents endangering the fertility of their lands. Not only do the farm workers suffer a loss of income, fishermen too find their traditional access to the sea cut off as the shrimp farms have laid huge inlet pumps to bring in sea water to fill the shrimp ponds.

The Bhagavati Environment Development Institute, Dindigul, claims that an analysis of water samples from half a dozen villages in Sirkazhi taluk had shown a disturbing degradation in the quality of groundwater. In each of the seven villages, shrimp farms, set up along the coast in the past two years, had wreaked havoc on the groundwater quality leading to serious environmental degradation.

The expert committee, constituted by the State Government in the wake of an agitation by farm labourers and fishermen against the setting up of shrimp farms on fertile lands, had suggested many a measure to regulate the growth of shrimp farms. But none of the suggestions appears to have been taken note of either by the shrimp farm promoters or the Government to surmount the challenges that agriculture has thrown upon farmers, corporate bodies and other government agencies.

7. Nylon Project in GOA and opposition from the local people

Controversy has raged over several development projects in Goa. One instance was the activities of the Zuari Agro Chemicals Ltd. Then there was public outcry over the danger to beaches by setting up of hotels. There was also strong protest against the Konkan Railway Project. Another project that has been under controversy is the Nylon 6,6 plant being set up by DuPont, a US multinational in collaboration with the Thapar Group (TDL). The project involved setting up a 18,500 tonnes per annum nylon cord plant at the Kerim plateau (30 km from the capital Panaji) with an investment of over Rs. 600 crores.

Following agitations, the then Progressive Democratic Front-ruled government appointed a House Committee to go into the environmental implications of the project. After a detailed and careful consideration of the issues involved, the Committee recommended that the project should be shelved on account of the likely threat of pollution. It called for the cancellation of the Letter of Intent. The Committee stated that "it would be an ill advised move to allow large chemical industries discharging even their 'treated' effluents in our ecorich and virgin rivers, ...we have to safeguard our rivers against any conceivable environment and pollution threat, ...while deciding on the establishment of large chemical industries in a small, relatively densely populated and socio-economically rich State such as ours, we should consider not only the statistical probability of a possible industrial accident but also the disastrous danger to human and ecology that may result from such an accident." However, the recommendations of the House Committee to shelve the project, not are taken seriously by the subsequent Congress (I) government.

The Anti-Nylon Citizen's Action Committee (ANCAC), headed by Dr. Dattaram Desai, which is spearheading the stir against the project said, "We will not under any circumstances, allow TDL to start operations in GOA" the ANCAC which came into being in October 1990 has launched an awareness campaign about the harmful effects of the project. Now there is nothing at the TDL site.

8. Chipko Movement

The Chipko (embrace) movement began in 1973 in the village of Mandal in the upper Alakananda valley under the leadership of Sri Chandi Prasad Bhatt ,a Sarvodaya leader from Dasauli Gram Swarajya Sang (DGSS). The DGSS was refused permission to use Ash trees for agricultural implements. After DGSS did all they could to protest, Bhatt, suddenly thought of embracing the trees. Women took their children to the forests and formed a circle around the trees to prevent the slaughtering of trees, The movement was so successful that the sport-goods manufacturing firm (Symonds and Company, Allahabad) was unable to cut down the allotted trees and their permit was cancelled. During the same year, the action of Chipko was re-enacted in Phata-Rampur area of the same district.

The Chipko protests in Uttar Pradesh achieved a major victory in 1980 with a 15 year ban on green felling in the Himalayan forests of that state by order of India's then Prime Minister Indira Gandhi. Since then the movement has spread to Himachal Pradesh in the North, Karnataka in the South, Rajasthan in the West, Bihar in the East and to the Vindhyas in Central India. In addition to the 15-year ban in Uttar Pradesh, the movement has stopped clear felling in the Western Ghats and the Vindhyas and generated pressure for a natural resource policy which is more sensitive to people's needs and ecological requirements.

The Chipko Movement is the result of hundreds of decentralised and locally autonomous initiatives. Its leaders and activists are primarily village women, acting to save their means of subsistence and their communities. Men are involved too, however, and some of these have given wider leadership to the movement. Prominent Chipko figures include : Sunderlal Bahuguna, a Gandhian activist and philosopher, whose appeal to Mrs. Gandhi resulted in the green-felling ban and whose 5,000 kilometer traverse—Himalaya footmarch in 1981-83 was crucial in spreading the Chipko message. Bahuguna coined the Chipko slogan : ecology is permanent economy.[1]

Sunderlal Bahuguna who joined the Chipko movement also opposed construction of Tehri dam. In 1989 he began the first of a series of hunger strikes to draw political attention to the dangers posed by the dam and in due course the Chipko Movement gave birth to the Save Himalaya Movement.

Thus, the Chipko movement (Gandhian method of Satyagraha nonviolent resistence) under followers of Chandi Prasad Bhatt and Sunderlal Bahuguna has been created to save the forests of India. It started out small but has grown over the years.

IMPLICATIONS FOR PUBLIC ADMINISTRATION

Environmental movements in our country and elsewhere do play a role of far-reaching importance in creating and achieving harmony between man and his environment on which his life and fate of future generation depend. These movements have largely influenced or even changed oppressive structures inimical to the development of the society. At the same time these movements are characterised by the political strength and creativity of the people in the struggle for qualitative change.

Acceptance has been growing regarding the interrelatedness between environment and development. However, the institutional and administrative supports to ensure sustainable development are largely lacking.

Responses to environmental movements frequently have entailed the adoption of environmental policies and statutes and the creation of a number of enforcement mechanisms. Overall, there is the need for a broader approach to public policy which entails focussing on improving the quality of environment. While state and central governments in India have long been accustomed to the administration of certain aspects of the environment, such as drinking water, sanitation and housing, a comprehensive approach to public administration is lacking. Strategies are needed which assure full cooperation between government and environmental groups and citizen groups and full participation of women in environmental administration. It is also imperative to develop and maintain a cadre of well-trained managers sensitive to the pressures of environmental movements.

Suggestions

1. Citizen participation is critical to enhancing the quality of environment and operation of public administration.
2. Cooperation with environmental movements' leaders is crucial in solving environmental crises.
3. Involvement of those directly affected by the environmental degradation must accompany work to bring about sound environmental change.
4. There is the need to develop capable managers who could be sensitive to the multidisciplinary nature of environmental administration.
5. The subject of environment management should find place in the domain of public administration for teaching and research purpose.

In brief, environmental movements in India can contribute substantially to the operation of public administration in an effective way. Their campaigns and meetings could provide valuable information to the public authorities for future policies. It is, therefore, vital to promote, strengthen and help environmental movements with a view to enchancing the quality of environment on which our own life depends.

Note

1. K. Siva Prasad and B. Ramachandra Yogi. Size, Structure and changing Role of the Indian Trade Unions. *The Indian Journal of Labour Economics*, Vol.37, No. 4, 1994, p. 765.

6

A PROGNOSIS ON THE PROBLEM OF ETHNIC UNREST IN INDIA

M. Venkat Reddy

The contemporary society is a complex one and has been changing rapidly, which is concomitant with a number of urges, demands, interests and obsessions. In view of this, in the present study, I would like to emphasise on various ethnic movements based with the Indian periphery : The activities of various organisations. In United Liberation Front of Assam (ULFA), Bodoland Autonomy Council (BAC), Jammu and Kashmir Liberation Front (JKLF), Jharkhand Mukti Morcha (JMM), Separate Telengana demand, separate Rayalaseema demand spearheading the movements with a view to "finding out some common basic issues or causes—whose 'remedies could be located in larger processes of development change and modernisation rather than with specific movements or organisations." In fact, the process of modernisation and development are caught up in the dialectics of their own dynamics. The ethnic conflict need to be viewed as part of an ongoing process, which have to be managed but can not be resolved once and for all except through the total assimilation or elimination of a particular group. But both are not so feasible options.

ETHNIC UNREST IN GENERAL

Ethnic movements connote an organised effort on the

part of an ethnic community for collective mobilisation to bring about changes in the socio-political system. Such a mobilisation by the ethnic leadership is in the main for greater access and control in the institutions of power and authority at various levels.

The emergence of ethnic movements can be attributed to many factors. First, to the gradual erosion or the tradition, normative framework and an increasing impetus to the ideologies of democracy, equality and distributive justice, with the perception and rejection of the ruling regimes as being discriminatory and oppressive, in ethnic terms. Such a linkage of ethnic consciousness occurs in the wider process of socio-economic changes in the polity.

In this respect, closely related to the erosion of the traditional normative framework is the invasion of the Western oriented package of urbanisation, industrialisation, Green Revolution and consumer culture dissemination which is transplanted in a developing / under developed region (as in the case of India) exacerbates structural distortions on the other.

Added to this is the increasingly interventionist role of the State and following from it, the penetration of State activities in the local realm. As and when the ever widening powers of the Centre as the epitome of integrating socio-cultural pluralities manifest in a virtually monolithic frame of nation state with the dominance of the majority ethnic group therein. The contradictions between state- building and a composite secular building of the nation surface, pave the way for ethnic movements.

The thrust of ethnicity is the manifestation of the increasing politicisation of the people and following from and mass politics striving to find avenues for a better life, the cultural identity anchoring. The mobilisation of such urges is reflected in social movements, ethnicity being one of the contenders for group protest and revolt in this respect.

The demands of ethnic movements have varied. In some cases, they have been for certain safeguards and reservations for the ethnic groups. In the main they have been for greater structural autonomy vis-a-vis the centre or within its constituent units i.e. the need for structural arrangements to provide political space for social pluralities.

However, over the decades, such autonomy demands have in many cases turned secessionist. Continued mismanagement by the ruling elite of the initial demands for linguistic accommodation, regional autonomy and iniquitous treatment in the sectors of education and employment have been some of the factors propelling autonomist movements to secessionism.

In the decades coming, caught between the quest for its ethnic roots and the gripping demands of the so-called modern state, mass politics is likely to become more and more ethnic. It is not because ethnicity provides greater distributive justice but because it has tremendous emotive appeal for such a projection. To such an extent, the demands / aspirations of the community are accommodated and contained through open, competitive and democratic processes, ethnicity has the potential to facilitate the composite process of nation building.

Ethnicity in search for communality

Having discussed ethnic unrests in various parts of the country, we have seen that as a phenomenon, ethnicity has evolved from historical and socio-territorial specificities which vary from area to area. Even so, underlying its stridence and its parted manifestations, certain common factors, implicit or imbibed in various unrests, can be discerned.

Uneven Development : Uneven development, both inter-regional and intra-regional, has contributed tremendously to the feeling of neglect, deprivation and of discrimination in many groups. This has been mainly because of highly centralised planning and capital intensive Nehruvian model of development. It brings out Centre's inability in meeting diverse needs of development as desired by various areas and groups. Inter-sectorial imbalances, as in the case of Punjab between agriculture and industry after green revolution, have also caused problems. Further more, highly skewed distribution of benefits of development over different social segments and groups has made certain groups feel left out in the process of raising the demand for separate districts, areas or state.

Under Development : Alongside the uneven development, is the problem of absolute under development. Thus many regions have no modern economic infrastructure and there is hardly any industrial activity. Consequently, there are little opportunities for the employment of educated youth who have high expectations. These educated unemployed youth provide ready made material to various organisations and movements. At times, despite area being richly endowed with natural resources, the potential has either not been tapped or the benefits have not accrued to the local people.

Politics of Opportunism and Manipulation : With politics losing its sense of purpose and the consequent degeneration of political process has greatly contributed to unrest. Thus we find that central leadership or mainstream political parties have manipulated ethnic symbols as much as others. It is a known secret how congress helped extremist section on Punjab to erode moderate Akali leadership and to divide the Akali party. And the result was Bhindranwale cult. Similarly, in Jammu & Kashmir, through unholy alliances, corrupt electoral practices, the political process lost all its credibility. And now we are struggling against all odds to start a political process afresh.

In North-Eastern region as well, it is a known fact that various political affiliations and individual leaders have supported and nurtured various terrorist and insurgent groups at various points of time to advance their personal or group political interest and to defeat their political opponents.

Frequent invocation of President's Rule, often on doubtful and partisan grounds, has also enforced imperialist image of the centre.

External dimension of Ethnic unrest : External support, both material and moral, has been very crucial for sustenance of ethnic movements in border areas. There lies the significance of geo-political periphery in relation to unrest in these areas. One can find it as a recurring factor in Punjab, J & K and North-Eastern States.

In the case of North-East, the geographical linkages coupled with the tribal affinities across the various union territories (at some point of time) and states in the region were such as to make militant group interaction feasible. Virtually unadministered Burmese tribal and hilly areas adjacent to the North-East have provided a haven to insurgents as well as relatively safe trekking route to China. An antagonistic pattern of bilateral relationship has equally a good opportunity for the separatists to look for a friend in the enemy's enemy. Pakistan, Bangladesh linkages with the North-Eastern Insurgents have clearly been discovered and traced. The China connections of the Nagas are well known.

In case of J&K, Pakistan's efforts are no more any secret. It has not left any stone unturned in giving support to various terrorist organisations in the valley. It provides training to terrorists, gives them sophisticated arms and ammunition, and provides them refuge.

Similarly, in case of Punjab, Pakistan and Sikh community abroad have played a tremendous role.

Enmeshed in the issue of material support is the factor of drug trafficking and smuggling. There has been an unholy ailiance between the extremists, smugglers and drug traffickers.

* Jharkhand provides a classic example in this regard. Some Afghani youths have also been caught in the Valley indulging in violence. They confessed that they have been sent by Pakistan.

Adhocism in Place of Long term Policy : The response of the centre in dealing with such movements has greatly been shaped by the personalities of the central leaders, ministers, the ruling party in the state. Even during long spells of President's rule, there has been no clear-cut sustained policy or any administrative will in this regard. Breakdown of consensus at national level, erosion of corporate cohesion at the centre after Nehru and often absence of a single united forum in the state of aggrieved group have definitely led to such a situation. Thus there are a number of terrorist organisations in Punjab, J&K and in North-East often pressing for the same demands notwithstanding internal division of opinion among the organisations.

Lackluster Performance of Government Officials : There has been a large gap between administrative goals and the actual performance of the administration. On the other hand, the expectations of people have been ever increasing. Apathy-insensitivity, and lack of commitment have led them to be seen only as agents of imperialist India. The communication gap between people and the government increased and left the field wide open for terrorist / insurgent groups to indulge in all kinds for propaganda. It has failed in tackling incipient insurgency and allowed events to assume crisis proportion. The government machinery has also been handicapped by many structural (e.g. absence of good intelligence network) and political constraints.

Historical Insulation in NE : Historical insulation of particular group with the centre is also a noteworthy and important factor in NE region. The people of North-Eastern region are not able to identify themselves with the plains men of other parts of India. Christian missionaries have played a major role in giving tribals separate identity leading to tribal national consciousness. One hopes that with advancement in transport and communication and with increasing needs of development there would be greater interaction, physical, social and cultural, removing the distance between minds of these two people.

Exploitation by Outsiders : Influx of outsiders in north-eastern states (both from within and outside the country) has caused perennial problems. It has altered the demography of the region often reducing the local population to minority giving way to an identity crisis. The more educated and skilled outsiders have taken a large chunk of already scarce opportunities and caused alienation of tribal people. The large scale immigration of manual population depressed the wages. The outsider businessmen and traders are seen as exploitators.

Non-implementation of Many Constitutional Provisions : Thus, one can see amidst divergent patterns of unrests, there are many similar elements. A sense of alienation of being discriminated of being neglected or deprived pervades all the groups. Demographic changes and peripheral status in mainstream culture make them apprehensive of losing their identity. A titled federal structure–not leaving enough constitutional space for separate entities to operate–and highly centralised economic planning failure to satisfy diverse needs of various groups are the macro factors. Force from across the border have provided sustenance and survival to many such groups. Failure of the administration to establish a psycho-emotional link with historically insulated population and consequently its failure to involve people in the development process and to redress their grievances, has been a major factor. The political power and the administration need to admit the failure on their part not with a spirit of accepting defeat but with a strength of introspection for preparing itself for the challenges waiting ahead.

Conclusion

In most of the cases, ethnic unrest is a manifestation of an individual's quest for a better life materially and culturally aggregated in a group. Historical factors have a major role in giving shape to unrest. The Indian system, with its institutions and policies, has not quite been able to cope up with the diverse demands of a pluralist society. It has been not able to satisfy the rising expectations of the people. And yet at the same time we have performed much better than many other countries in this respect.

In the wake of our analysis of various movements, we feel that the system must correct itself in many ways in the following direction.

- The most urgent need is that the political leaders, both at centre and state level and administrative functionaries at higher level become serious and display an enlightened sense of commitment and duty towards the country.
- The process has to be in consultation with and in accordance with the needs of the people. Thus it must be seen that knowledge and skills of the population are improved so that they derive meaningful benefits from economic activities rather than being exploited by it. Human resource development has to be emphasised. Regional imbalances, which have been subject of controversy in the recent times and perhaps main source of demand for autonomy of groups on a particular region have to be checked.
- Administration must realise its historical role in these areas. Not only that it has to provide a mechanical presence of government but also a government with heart and soul. It must contact masses, remove their grievances and fears. It must faithfully implement the policies and programmes prepared for these areas.
- Ethnic violence is a manifestation of a deeper malaise in the system. Simultaneous administrative and political actions are essential.
- The peace in Punjab for the time being, provides from violence and provides the centre an opportunity to genuinely solve its problems. At the same time administration has to exploit this atmosphere of peace to build up credibility with the people and improve its hold.

- The Centre should lay down a clear cut policy which should be communicated to various levels of administration. Considering the moral and material support, these movements enjoy from across the border, India should improve its bilateral relations with its neighbours. It should also utilise other international for a to put pressure on these countries aiding and at the same time abetting terrorism.

7

TRADE UNION MOVEMENT AND THE NEW ECONOMIC POLICY

V. Bhaskara Rao and T.V. Sujatha Kumari

Trade Unions have almost become inevitable in every enterprise, irrespective of size, business, ownership and geographical location. The most important contribution of union movement is the increased attention paid to 'human factors' in the industry[1]. Trade Unions have influenced the course of economic activity and development throughout the world from the time of their emergence. In advanced capitalist countries, trade unions have fought against exploitation and later settled down to the promotion of economic interests of workers. But in socialist countries, their role has been supplementary but subordinate to the state and political party in ensuring the production targets of enterprises. They also have to look after the labour interests. There was no apparent conflict among the goals of labour, industry and state.

In developing democratic countries which have chosen the middle path of mixed economy, trade unions are perceived as labour institutions that not only promote the interests of labour but also contribute to the socioeconomic transformation of the economy and the society. More specifically, trade union movement can help in the progress of developing countries like India, by paying attention to workers, industry and economy[2].

The primary function of the movement is to secure workers interests like wages, job security, better working conditions and other facilities. Over the sixty last years, after many struggles, there is commendable improvement in the condition of labour in business, industry, agriculture and services. But the Indian economy was in shape for the severe economic crisis in 1990. The International Monetary Fund and World Bank were willing to help with their conditionalities. They are causing serious problems for the poverty stricken people as well as working people, even in the organised sectors[3]. The New Economic Policy announced by the Government of India in 1991 has certain adverse implications for the workers. It may be emphasised that human resources development and social care find no place of importance in the New Economic Policy. Keeping this in view, the paper discusses some issues concerning trade union movement in India vis-a-vis the on-going economic reforms in India.

The new economic policies have far reaching implications on the future of trade union movement in India[4]. The traditional role of protecting the workers from arbitrary treatment will be no more the main concern and issue. The Industry is primarily concerned with excelling in the highly competitive global environment. The use of latest technology, which is essential today, has considerably reduced the role of mass production worker with adverse impact on the unions.

The Government introduced New Economic and Industrial Policies having a bearing on Trade Union movement. The implications and the reaction of Trade Union movement on some of the important policies are analysed below :

1. Closure of Industrial Units, Exit Policy and the National

Renewal Fund : The Government announced that the chronically sick public sector units would be referred to the

Board of Industrial and Finance Reconstruction (BIFR). On its recommendation many such units would be closed down and a social security package would be created to protect the interest of the retrenched workers. In order to minimise the adverse impact of structural adjustment on the level of employment and labour conditions, the Government formulated the "Exit Policy"[5]. It allows employers to retrench their surplus staff and to close down their loss, making plants and enterprises.

Since rendering workers out of job means playing with their lives, for which there was stiff opposition to this decision of Government not only from the affected workers but also from the Trade Union movement, irrespective of the political affiliation. Essentially, their stance was that the entire policy package was anti working class and therefore not acceptable to them.

The trade union leaders demanded that the Exit Policy would be accepted only if the workers are immediately absorbed in other profit making enterprises. The National Renewal Fund (NRF) which was created to provide retrenchment compensations to the workers, does not at all, according to them, specify any concrete measures towards this end. It only made provision for golden handshake, which was not only unacceptable to the union leaders and even the fund will be insufficient to meet the one time needs of all the retrenched workers.

2. Privatisation and Disinvestment of the Public Sector Units

Government of India announced a policy of offering part of the governments share holding in the Public Sector to the mutual funds, financial institutions, the general public and the workers. This would further curtail the size and scope of the Public Sector. Along with the policy for closing down the sick public sector units, the profit making units also, in phased manner, get out of the control of the Public Sector.

Most of the trade unions consistently opposed to privatisation. This belief stems from their ideology of sharing of gains by all, including the workers, privatisation pampers capitalists who for ages, in the eyes of the union leaders, have been exploiting the workers. The Government also adopted the socialistic pattern of society and privatisation was discouraged with a large number of regulations and licenses. The new policies gave a clear message that the future of Indian Industry would be in the hands of the private sector.

The Trade Union's claim launching an industry in the private sector is no guarantee that the unit will always be productive and contribute positively to the economy of the country. The union leaders are against disinvestment in the public sector units and privatisation is also due to the fact that the Government will no longer have the power to direct investment to any end of the public policy.

3. Foreign Investment and Multinationals

The Government of India approved for direct investment up to 51 per cent equity in high priority industries. Even hundred per cent foreign equity has been allowed in certain key industries with total export orientation. Many export policies related to trade have been taken up to facilitate foreign investment and the entry of multinationals in India.

The Trade Unions fear that opening the flood gates to foreign investment and multinationals cause unemployment since these units bring in sophisticated technology which require less manpower[6].

Multinationals adversely affect employment in small scale units (B.S. Dhume, AITUC) and can not compete in quality. One of the Conveners of the Trade Union solidarity felt that, "the MNC's will only come and exploit our cheap labour, sell obsolete technology and drain foreign exchange" (Vasudevan). The CITU union leaders said that "local monopolies will get together with collaborators and eat the cream (Bajaj, H.L).

4. Delicensing and MRTP Act

The Government of India announced delicensing of most of the industries and amendments to remove the threshold limits of assets in respect of MRTP companies and dominant undertakings. Since the licensing policy of the government was considered to be one of the major obstacles to the growth of Indian industries as well as the entry of multinationals, the measures were welcomed by almost all.

The Trade Unions, however felt that the licensing policy of the government helped in investing in the areas which were crucial for the country along with locating them in the backward rural areas. The amendments to the MRTP Act are also criticised by the union leaders on the ground that these will result in concentration of wealth in the hands of the few, thus further widen income disparities in India. The unions demanded a comprehensive package and rejected the Government's offer 'of 45 days salary for every retrenched workers. Thus New Economic Policy created insecurity and uneasiness in the Indian labour class and posed a major threat to the Trade Union rights of the working people.

Indian Trade Union Movement at Cross Roads

Trade Union Movement since independence made rapid strides. It has been able to prevent exploitation of the working class and build a strong base in the organised sector. It has also been able to mobilise white-collar workforce including the public sector employees. But to day it has been attacked from all sides. As such, its very survival as the representative body of working class is at stake[7]. The major challenges faced by the Trade Union movement are analysed below.

Issues for Trade Union Movement:

The Trade Union movement in India, which is over a century old, is now facing, as elsewhere in the world, major changes and challenges[8].

Economic reforms accentuated the problems that the workers were already facing. It is realised that "sub-

Table 1

Impact of Economic Reforms on Trade Unions

SL NO.	REFORM MEASURES	IMPACT ON INDUSTRY & ECONOMY	IMPACT ON UNION MOVEMENT	SUGGESTED MEASURES
1	Globalisation	Entry of more MNCs	Pressure on unions and weakening of union Power	Collaboration with international organisations like ICFTU & ILO
2.	Intensification of competition	Closures and Industrial sickness	Decline in union membership, pressure on unions.	Organising the unorganised alternative forms of ownership like workers 'cooperatives; mobilisation of more finances; more fraternal activities like training for self-employment; training for self-employment; and management of funds.
3.	Privatisation Measures	More sub-contracting, Flexi-employment; Casualisation of labour	Decline in membership Weakening of union movement; Pressure on Unions power;	
4.	Changes in the industrial relations system	Less State role: more bilateralism; Culture of dominance on the part of employers/ management	Weakening of union; Pressure on Central Unions	Constructive cooperation with management; strengthening of unions at plant level.
5.	Resort to high technology; modernisation;	Job losses; Adverse effect on women and unskilled labour; Rise of professional/ technical labour	Emergence of non-unions decline of union membership	Organisational changes in unions to mobilisae emerging labour classes; Working for macro policy changes on rationalisation and social security.
6.	Strategic cooperation between a. Governement and business b. Firms	Joint Ventures Foreign collaboration Mergers and takeovers	Weakening of union-power pressure for knowledge and information	Collaboration among unions at local, regional, industrial national and international levels; mergers among union unity and solidarity measures.

Source: S.K.G Sundarm; Economic Reforms and The Future of Indian Trade Union Movement; The Indian Journal of Labour Economics, Vol. 39, No.4, 1996.

contracting, automation, VRS and contract labour" will pose new challenges[9]. The impact of economic reforms on Trade Union movement and the suggested measures to face the emerging adverse impact on labour are indicated in a schematic presentation in Table 1.

Trade Union Movement against New Economic Reforms

Labour movement in India opposed the implementation of New Economic and Industrial policies which have generated economic tensions among the working class. Trade Unions protested against New Economic Reforms. There was some unity and consensus among the trade unions in interpreting the 'new' economic and industrial policies as being anti-working class in as much as some of the policies were perceived to have adverse effects on employment, earning etc. Three nation wide 'bandhs' were organised during 1991 and 1992. The left trade unions conducted show downs against the governments' New Economic Policy. Nation-wide strikes, general strikes were also organised. The nation-wide strike on November 29, 1991 was the first major show of force by the trade unions. The BMS observed a "Warning Week" from June 8, 1992, during which its cadres organised demonstrations and gate meetings. Its warning was against the free entry of multinational corporations and other aspects of the new policy that undermine self-reliance. The new demands of the trade unions at that time, which agitated against the government's new economic policy are[10]:

1. Scrap the New Industrial Policy.
2. Reverse all "IMF-Inspired" economic policies.
3. Abandon privatisation and Public economic policies.
4. Put an end to closures and retrenchments.
5. Stop the entry of multinationals.
6. Revive all sick units.
7. Bring down prices.

8. Raise minimum wages for unorganised sector.
9. Introduce genuine land reforms and
10. End discrimination of women workers.

Another nation-wide strike was organised on 16 June, 1992 by the trade unions in which the INTUC did not participate. Left-led trade union federations and Hind Mazdoor Sabha organised a massive rally and threatened to hold a Bharat Bandh if the government did not reverse its "anti-labour" policies. Even the trade union wing of the party in power, the Indian National Trade Union Congress had, in November 1992, given a one-month's ultimatum on the subject. Most trade unions, including the INTUC, raised for several demands which put the ambivalent government in a quixotic position. On most aspects, the government did not politically seem inclined to say no and yet unwilling to readily agree for fear of being forced to follow-up. Given the vulnerability of the unions, the attitude of the Government seem to satisfy them than be confronted with a hard 'no'. The trade unions demands include:[11]

1. **Finalising the issue of Dearness Allowance :** The Government's acceptance of the Fourth Central Pay Commission recommendations on Central Dearness Allowance opened the pandora's box. Ever since, the Government's attitude towards industrial dearness allowance is weakened politically, morally and legally. The Supreme Court, R.B. Mishra Committee, Tripartite DA Committee, Ramanujam Committee, Ministerial committee and the Ray Committee, have dealt or continued to deal with this issue. Rather than untangle the vaxatious issues, simultaneous reference to more than one committee and frequent assurances and public statements added to the complexity. Whispers about the question of freezing DA had to be emphatically denied by the concerned ministers for fear of political fall out.

2. In several countries where the IMF and the world Bank initiated structural adjustment reforms, wage freeze

and D.A. freeze were applied. But unions in India were successful, thus far, in getting an assurance from the Government that there would be no wage freeze or DA freeze.

3. Continued budgetary support to public sector units referred to the BIFR.
4. Lifting the ban on commencing negotiations in public enterprises where collective agreements have expired.
5. Candid assurance that there would be no exit policy.
6. Retraining, redeployment and Voluntary Retirement Scheme to avoid retrenchment.
7. Three-fold increase in retrenchment compensation for workers in case of closure of industrial units.
8. Immediate implementation of the pension scheme whereever agreements in this regard have been reached.
9. Abolish or rise the salary eligibility limit for purposes of bonus.
10. Raise the salary exemption limit for income tax.

The Committee of Public Sector Trade unions (CPSTU), the apex body of Public Sector workers submitted a memorandum to the Union Government on June 22, 1994 against the Government's policy on Public Sector and its negative attitude towards revival of sick public sector units[12]. It expressed firm commitment to defend the Public Sector at any cost and declared its readiness to extend all support to any move to strengthen public sector network :

1. The Government shares the responsibility of revival of sick public sector units.
2. Public Sector units are not discriminated in the matter of orders and are regularly fed with orders to ensure full capacity utilisation.
3. Disinvestment of shares of PSUs is stopped.

4. Public Sector units are not starved of funds for purchase of raw material. And
5. The Government permits the Public Sector managements to workout viability proposals jointly with the trades unions in the interest of the country's economy and all concerned.

Such blanket opposition from the entire movement, however, did not deter the Government. The Government could confidently go ahead with its policy despite opposition from the Trade Union movement.

Indian Trade Union Movement is deeply fragmented along many lines. This is one of the major reasons why it failed to assert itself in the context of the New Economic policy. At one level, the movement is divided along political lines with each political party having its own trade union wing. Caught up in their own petty rivalries, the organisations failed to see the common issues affecting the working class in general.

At another level, the movement is atomised because of the growth of enterprise level unions. Efforts to bring these unions under one umbrella have not been successful because they lack a common ideological basis that can bind them together. Given such deep fragmentation within the movement, it is not surprising that the trade union response to NEP has been so diffused and ineffective. 35th National Convention of AITUC at Patna felt that there should be one union in an establishment, one industrial federation at state and national levels, and one central trade union at the national level which would function democratically and independently. But the CITU ruled out the proposal for merger of central trade unions as an 'impracticable step'.

For establishing industrial peace, the Government gave an elaborate legal system to workers instead of a "Collective bargaining procedure". This was altogether detrimental to working class solidarity. It sank the trade union movement into the deep dark ocean of legal procedures and technical jurisprudence. This involvement in legal affairs smashed the revolutionary dynamism of the labour movement and it was impossible for unions to develop their leadership for future struggles. Bureaucracy also played a significant role in ousting trade unions from participating in decision-making process.

Another trend observed in trade union movement is that the struggles of the organised sector of the workers and employees evoke so little sympathy among other sections of the people. Such lack of sympathy is partly due to the motivated propaganda of the ruling classes to isolate the organised sector of workers and employees. But it has to be acknowledged that the orientation of Trade Union movement strongly biased towards the relatively privileged sections of the workforce has to an extent helped the Government in its divisive game of pitting one section of working class against the another.

It is evident from the Kanoria Jute Mill case, the the modus operandi of the left government towards trade unions is substantially different when it is in power than without. Since the assumption of office by the left front, class struggle in West Bengal, has been ignored[13].

Future Perspectives

Based on the experience since independence including the period of reforms, Trade Unions must chalkout their strategy for the future. Some of the areas where Trade Unions should pay attention is given below :

1. Trade Unions must have a debate among themselves and at the other relevant forums on the weakness and shortcomings of the Trade Union Movement which have been hindering its developmental role.
2. Trade Unions should form a confederation as, in Australia, Japan, Sweden etc., such Confederations, known as Australian Trade Union Congress (ACTU), Japanese Trade Union Confederation (RENGO),

Swedish Trade Union confederation are more effective. Since they could also become partners to centralised collective bargaining mechanisms.

3. Trade Unions should keep links with political practices but they should not adopt in general their ideology.
4. Trade Unions must be aware that in a changing world coercive methods can be avoided.
5. Trade Unions need to pay attention to their membership in the future for their survival and expansion.
6. To ensure effectiveness of Trade Unions 'workers education' scheme must be restructured to suit the changing environment in the country.
7. In the changed environment, a new approach to labour management relations is needed. When reforms usher in, much more co-operation for production and productivity is needed between Trade Unions and management in order to survive and succeed together in the markets characterised by gloablisation, privatisation, liberalisation, free trade and free payment system. Trade Unions have to transform themselves into agents of change for bringing benefits to workers and society.
8. Trade Unions to be effective at the economy level must develop a common forum and achieve unity.
9. Information on research in areas which can affect labour is necessary in the prevailing environment.
10. Trade Unions have to actively participate in the revival of sick units because closures affect the workers most.
11. Trade Unions should monitor the human situation, especially of living standards etc. of not only their members but also of poor, with regard to healthy nutrition.
12. "Adjustment policies should form an integral part of a longer term vision and development strategy and, as

such sociological and ecological context"[14]. Such national policies require the popular support of all social actors including the Trade Unions. Trade Unions should influence and be willing to be influenced to put in place desired and feasible policies.

Trade Unions must realise that it is not enough to denounce public policies. It is equally important to generate effective alternatives with regard to each of the above and such other aspects considered significant and relevant in this context and widely disseminate them for gaining popular support.

CONCLUSION

Trade Union movement in India is passing through difficult times due to implementation of new policies which have generated economic tensions among the working class. Protests against New Economic Reforms have become part and parcel of Trade Union Movement. India's liberalisation as also globalisation of its market is having direct effect on employment conditions as increasing number of jobs are being subcontracted. The Government, as regulating body, has not been much supportive of Trade Union Movement and this is indicated by the fact that no constructive amendments to various labour legislations in tune with existing conditions have so far realised. To an ordinary worker the whole environment seems to be hostile and he, despite of being represented by Trade Unions, finds himself in a helpless situation.

In order to meet the challenges thrown up by IMF- World Bank dictated economic reforms, both CITU and AITUC seem intent on finding new forms of struggles to channelise the growing discontentment of the working class, no new model appeared to have evolved from the movements waged by these central Trade Unions. It goes without saying that Trade Union leadership cannot, by themselves, discover new forms of struggle.

The need of the hour is that the Trade Unions should seriously fight against vested interests whose main objective is to deunionise workers. At the same time, they should self critically examine their role and responsibility in alienating the workers. The Trade Unions should take corrective measures in order to build a united movement for promoting and protecting worker interests.

Notes

1. S.K.G. Sundaram. Trade Unions As Labour Institutions and their Role in India's Socio-economic Transformation. *Indian Journal of Labour Economics*, Vol. 36, No. 4, 1993, p. 898.
2. Shanti Patel. New Economic Policy, Its impact on Workers: Industrial Restructuring and Surplus Labour Rehabilitation in G.S. Saxena & J.S. Narayana Rao (Editors), Delta Publishing House, Delhi, 1995, p. 3.
3. J.S. Sodhi. New Economic Policies And their Impact on Industrial Relations, *Indian Journal of Industrial Relations*, Vol. 29, No. l, July, 1993, p. 33.
4. For details see, T.V. Sujatha Kumari, New Economic Policy and Its impact on Trade Unions And Workers, in S.K. Singh (ed), Public Sectors In India, Rawat Publications, New Delhi, 1997, pp. 256-265.
5. J.S. Sodhi. New Economic Policies And their Impact on Industrial Relations, *Indian Journal of Industrial Relations*, Vol. 29, No. l, July, 1993. p. 40.
6. Pravin Singa. Indian Trade Unionism at Cross Roads. *The Indian Journal of Labour Economics*, Vol. 3, No. 37, 1994, p. 771.
7. C.S.Venkata Ratnam. Impact of New Economic Policy on the Role of Trade Unions, *Indian Journal of Industrial Relations*, Vol. 29, No. l, July, 1993, p. 55.
8. S.K. Sundaram. Economic Reforms and the Future of Indian Trade Union Movement, *The Indian Journal of Labour Economics*, Vol. 39, No. 4, 1996, p. 1070.

9. "Deccan Chronicle", Secunderabad, June 10, 1992, p. 13.
10. C.S. Venkataratnam. *op.cit.*, p. 68.
11. S.S.Tiwana, Trade Union Movement In India : Emerging Trends, *The Indian Journal of Labour Economics*, Vol. 37, No. 4, 1994.
12. S.S. Tiwana. *op.cit*, p. 745.
13. S.C. Venkataratnam. op.cit, p.72.

8

LOK SATTA (PEOPLE POWER)

V. Bhaskara Rao

Lok Satta is a non-partisan citizens initiative and peoples movement for democratic reforms launched by Foundation for Democratic Reforms (FDR).[1] Lok Satta believes that the existing political impasse needs a "creative, innovative and democratic" response, in order to help the nation overcome the larger governance crisis. For an honest and stable government, certain suitable major reforms in the constitution are required. To bring such reforms building national consensus and generating a debate to create public opinion is felt necessary.

According to Lok Satta, India is racing an extraordinary crisis of governance due to :

Inefficient state, increasing lawlessness, competitive populism, criminalisation of polity, ever-growing nexus between money power, crime and political power, excessive centralisation, marginalisation of people in the political and governance process, endemic corruption, extremely tardy and inefficient justice system and erosion of legitimacy and authority.

The diagnosis of the causes of the malady is too exhaustive and too evident to every one. Lok Satta demands honest, purposive governance with full participation of the people with effective systems ensuring transparency, accountability, efficiency and responsiveness.

Lok Satta feels that unless there is a concerted effort to improve the rules of the political game and make our governance truly democratic, the crisis cannot be resolved. For this purpose, Lok Satta advocates genuine electoral reforms to make election an honest and effective expression of people's will and to make the legislatures effective. The followings are some of the measures suggested for immediate reforms:

(i) Internal democracy in political parties with respect to elections for leadership, and choice of candidates:

(ii) Election Reforms as suggested by Dinesh Goswamy Committee and Election Commission.

(iii) Freedom of Information to citizens in all matter pertaining to governance.

(iv) Independent, transparent mechanism for appointment of all constitutional functionaries.

(v) A strong constitutional institution to combat corruption, with adequate powers, and complete control over anti corruption wings of admmistration.

(vi) A genuine local governance system providing for a third tier of governance with a separate local government list of subjects under the 7th schedule, and removing some of the anomalies in the 73rd amendment (for instance, delinking the three tiers of Panchayats).

(vii) Repeal of, or amendments to Article 356, to make its application fair, transparent and non-partisan.

(viii) Independent method to appointment of State Governors with security of tenure.

(ix) Civil Service Boards to monitor and decide on all postings and transfers of permanent public servants, ensuring tenure of office for all key public offices.

(x) Practical measures for speedy justice as recommended in Law Commission reports.

Organisational Structure of Lok Satta

Lok Satta is an open organisation, came into existence on 3rd August 1997. Any citizen, who is not a member of any political party can seek membership in Lok Satta by paying Rs 10/- towards ordinary annual membership or Rs. 100/- towards life membership. Lok Satta is at present organised in A P. The members at different levels elect from their units and elect their executive. According Lok Satta at state level, district level, mandal level and village level units are formed. In the beginning, District Coordination Committees are formed for campaign of Lok Satta's ideals. Lok Satta functions democratically at each level. (No nominations) and at each level lower tiers will have representation and decision-making power.

Lok Satta's main objective is to launch national campaign for democratic reforms through public awareness. It preaches that people are the masters and the rulers are the servants and people are paramount, the real decision making powers must be vested with the people. Lok Satta believes in the reforms for genuine democratisation of political process, effective decentralisation of governance, the empowerment of citizens, debureaucratisation of administration and creation of speedy, efficient, affordable and accessible justice system.

The crisis of Indian State according to Lok Satta is mainly because of two flaws in the governance structure:

1. Good behaviour is not rewarded and bad behaviour is not checked or punished.
2. The nature of power and its exercise could be able to achieve only about 15 to 20 per cent of its capacity.

Due to the flaws, the nation faces three dangers :

1. Increasing lawlessness and anarchy in most parts.
2. The possibility of despotism by invitation.
3. The spectre of balkanisation.

The present Indian State is evaluated in terms of the ingredients of democracy on an imaginary scale of 0 to 100. India's score is shown in the following chart.

Chart - I
Ingredients of Indian Democratic State

S. No.	Ingredient	Scale (0-100)
1.	Freedom (Individual)	60-90
2.	Self-Governance	25
3.	Empowerment	5-10
4.	Rule of Law	Almost Nil
5.	Self Correction	Almost Zero

It is identified that the Indian crisis is systemic and constitutional, Therefore, the way out is recognised as holistic, peaceful and democratic transformation of Indian Republic, with the following objectives:

"building at all levels of free, self-governing empowering, self- correcting institutions, capable of maintaining peace and harmony, preserving order and stability, strengthening unity and integrity, enabling freedom and participation and promoting growth and prosperity",

Reforms Agenda of Lok Satta

1. Democratisation of political parties.
2. Separation of Executive and Legislative.
3. Safeguards against executive abuse.
4. Decentralisation of governance.
5. Efficient and responsive bureaucracy.
6. Speedy and efficient justice system.

1. Democratisation of political parties

Lok Satta traces many of the ills of Indian governance system to the undemocratic and unaccountable functioning of the political parties. It is observed that their internal functioning is "arbitrary, autocratic, undemocratic, invisible and unaccountable". Parties in India function like private estates, the election process becoming a competitive game among closed oligarchies to grab political power and control the state resources. Therefore, Lok Satta strongly believes that the first major area of reform is democratisation of political parties in certain matters like:

1. Membership.
2. Internal democracy.
3. Selection of candidates for elective public office.
4. Political and campaign funding.
5. Electoral Reforms.

On every aspect of the reform proposed, Lok Satta suggested a number of clear and relevant points which are really desirable.

2. Separation of Executive and Legislature

Dr. Jayaprakash Narayan, personally, is of the opinion that the West Minister Model practised in India over the past sixty years severely undermined the legitimacy of authority and effectiveness of executive functioning due to several distortions crept into the Indian Parliamentary system.

In the existing system, all governance is reduced to patronage. There is a well-developed market for public office in India, with the exclusion of people from the political process or governance; most are sullen, resentful, angry and frustrated. The local public servant behaves as always corrupt, greedy, arrogant and arbitrary. Despite the change of governments and parties, public protests, demonstration and at time violence, the real character of governance does not seem any change.

Under the circumstances, the ministers don't have any, either common purpose, larger vision or understanding of public affairs. They are very often a bunch of warring tribes, perpetually feuding for crumbs of office or to further their group interests. Finally, the unsuitable constitutional land legal mechanisms that were evolved lend the Indian republic in an extraordinary crisis of governability.

It is important to note that a large and important part of people's lives is neither touched by the government nor are the people given control over the government to guide their own destinies. Increasingly, today Indian polity has become a dysfunctional anarchy.

3. Safeguards Against Executive Abuse

Perpetuation of the same functionaries (Ministers and Higher Officials) for long in high public office at various executive levels tended to undermine democratic institutions. The oath of secrecy taken by every minister and the obsessive secrecy in government functioning at various levels have alienated people from governance. Therefore, the following suggestions are made:

1. Limitation on term and tenure of office.
2. Guaranteed right to information.
3. Independent crime investigation and prosecution.
4. Independent appointment of constitutional functionaries like Judges, Election Commission, C&AG etc at local, district and national level.
5. Direct election of the chief executive.

4. Decentralisation of Governance

Due to high centralisation there is no true self-governance. Therefore, there must be restructuring on the following aspects:

1. The Centre-State relations must be comprehensively re-negotiated, establishing true and effective federalism.
2. There must be genuine local governance system to ensure people's participation.
3. There must be effective empowerment of people as stakeholders.

5. Reorienting Federalism

The following reforms are suggested in Federal Polity :

1. Repealing of Article 356—The Centre cannot dismiss any state government
2. Directly elected governor to simultaneously function as head of state and head of government.
3. Revision of distribution of powers in favour of state governments in three lists: Union list, State list and Local government list and No Concurrent list.
4. Fiscal devolution by fixed percentage of all revenues of the union to the states.
5. Creation of new Indian Judicial Service and dispensing with the existing All India Services.
6. Reforms in Local Self-Governance-local elected executive must have complete control over all the matters including the local bureaucracy.
7. Direct empowerment of stakeholders to change to create nexus between the vote and the welfare of citizens and linking authority with accountability.

6. Efficient and Responsive Bureaucracy

In India the public servant is transformed into the master and the citizen become the subject. The extraordinary degree of lifetime security given to every government servant with no chance of punishing him made it impossible for good governance. Further, due to political populism and direct subsidies, the government servant became a giver and the citizen a receiver, promoted corruption and it reversed the votes between the master and the servant. Arbitrary transfers and postings demoralised the civil services Therefore, bureaucratic reforms are recommended to make more efficient and responsive.

Second Freedom Struggle

Lok Satta gave call for Second Freedom Struggle for what

India achieved in 1947, was only transfer of power. Now it is time to achieve the true freedom through organised concerted action with effective networking. Lok Satta published a volume in Telugu on "Second Freedom Struggle": A call by Lok Satta: consisting of about 100 pages. It is almost freely distributed. In this book about 21 issues are thoroughly discussed: the objectives of Lok Satta at different levels, and the role of the members of Lok Satta in A.P. How to struggle against corruption, the publicity mechanism, national study groups to study and recommended on various issues (about 60 issues are identified) etc. It is almost a manual of Lok Satta-consisting of rules, Dos and Don'ts.

Swarajya-Peoples Charter

Swarajya movement is aimed at making governments and their agencies accountable to people. It reclaims the people's republic, which has been robbed by a small group of politicians and government servants and wants to reassert the people's sovereignty. Swarajya movement launched by Lok Satta has four components:

1. Peoples Charter.
2. Public broadcasting capsules.
3. Citizen's neighborhood watch groups.
4. Select and demonstration campaigns.

People's charter is a powerful tool to empower the citizens: like certificates, land related issues, public distribution system, voting rights, civic issues, public utilities, civil rights and stake-holders empowerment.

On each issue covered (60 issues are stated) information is given on the following.

1. What should a citizen do to get a particular service?
2. What is the government Agency expected to do. What is the procedure to follow?
3. What are the reasonable performance standards for each service?

4. What can a citizen do when the government agency fails to deliver the service?

Election Watch

Election Watch is a programme sponsored by Lok Satta during 1998 mid-term poll to Lok Sabha and the programme is renewed during the General election in 1999. Election Watch programme is aimed at enlightening the electorate on the need for healthy and democratic process in India with an objective of reforms in the electoral system.

Election Watch committees are formed with credible and non-partisan citizens from a more than 10 Professions. At the state level there is a broad-based committee and a core group to guide and monitor Election Watch activities at District and Constituency level Election Watch Committees.

A detailed and very exhaustive informative book entitled "Election Watch Movement, 1999" was published by Lok Satta, consisting of about 90 pages with R.K. Lakshmans cartoons and providing everything about elections and what the Election Watch Committees have to do.

Lok Satta organised a highly successful Election Watch during the 1998 Lok Sabha elections. In 35 parliamentary constituencies, common platforms were organised with intense public participation and media coverage. 'Know your candidate and 'Enroll and vote campaign' was mounted effectively. In the light of the experience of 1998, Election Watch 1999 has been chalked out with clarity and precision.

The Activities of Election Watch Movements

1. Verification of Electoral Rolls

- Obtaining Electoral Rolls constituency-wise, and polling station-wise,
- Verification of Electoral Rolls with the help of local people, and identification of names that should be included or deleted or changed.

- Help citizens to file applications for inclusion or deletion using the appropriate forms.

2. Screening of Potential Candidates

- Preparation of lists of potential candidates of major parties.
- Verification of antecedents, with respect to criminal record and corruption.
  - Press reports.
  - Formal Changes.
  - Convictions.
  - Wide notoriety.
  - Police records like history sheets, rowdy sheeters etc.
- Publicizing record.
- Pressure on political parties not to select persons with known corrupt or criminal record.

3. Electoral Reforms Agenda at the Election Commission Level

- Focus on easy reforms that can be implemented by the Election Commission without any change of law.
- Build Consensus.

4. Know your Candidate

- Questionnaire to all Candidates.
- Political record.
- Criminal involvement.
- Financial status and assets.
- Views on policies and governance reforms.
- Wide publicity.
- Public opportunity to opponents to challenge the veracity of information furnished.

5. Common Platform

- Common public debate.
- Structural platform with an impartial moderator.
- Brief opening statements of candidates.
- Response to written questions.
- Brief closing statements.
- Wide media coverage.

6. Enroll and Vote Campaign

- Wide disseminationed information on verification and enrollment.
- Radio and TV campaign to promote voting.
- Appeal to choose candidates without criminal and corrupt record.
- Invalidate the vote if no candidate is preferred, instead of staying at home (to prevent impersonation and to record protest)

List of Publications of Lok Satta

1. The Indian Republic – Collapse and Rejuvenation, 1997.
2. Harnessing People's Power for Rejuvenation of our Republic, A Discussion Paper, June, 1997 (English and Telugu).
3. Second Freedom Struggle, November, 1997 (Telugu Mannual).
4. Swarajya: People's character, Sept, 1998, (Telugu and English).
5. Election Watch Movement, 1999 (Telugu).
6. Political Parties and Indian Democracy, 1998.
7. Jana Balam – Monthly News Letter.
8. A Number of booklets, leaflets and circulars.

Note

1. Foundation for Democratic Rights FDR is a registered society, came into existence in 1997. FDR is voluntary association formed with the objective of promotion of "holistic, peaceful, democratic transformation of Indian Polity". It was founded by Dr. Jaya Prakash Narayana and others. Dr. Jayaprakash Narayan, formerly, was reputed as sincere and honest IAS Officer, served as the Secretary to Governor of AP and N.T. Rama Rao, the Chief Minister of A.P. before he resigned his job. FDR prepared a Discussion Paper written by Dr. Jaya Prakash Narayan entitled "Lok Satta Strategy for Rejuvenation of Indian republic" 1997 (123 pages). He extensively toured many districts, addressed many Seminars, met a number of eminent people, and discussed with cross section of intellectuals for a period of one year. The result of his discussions made to realise to establish a People's Organisation called. 'Lok Satta'.

9

TEACHING OF PUBLIC ADMINISTRATION IN A.P. *

A. Vijay Kumar

Public Administration is a young discipline in India, yet its advancement over a period of few decades has been impressive. Public Administration education has been gradually expanding. Today the subject is taught in more than 50 universities in the country. Thousands of students have obtained their Undergraduate and Post-graduate degrees in Public Administration. Hundreds of scholars have obtained research degrees in the discipline and several others have chosen this subject for their career. The subject is also taught in the training courses for civil servants. The public personnel recruitment agencies are also offering this discipline in competitive examinations. Thus, the importance of Public Administration discipline has been growing day by day.

An attempt is made to present the opinions of teachers and students of Public Administration on the teaching of Public Administration discipline in the universities and colleges of Andhra Pradesh. To obtain the opinions of the teachers and students, a structured questionnaire was administered on 200 undergraduate, 100 postgraduate students and 100 teachers selecting them from different

*Paper Presented to the VIII National Conference of NEPASI organised by IIPA, New Delhi during the November 25, 26-2005.

regions of Andhra Pradesh. The opinions expressed by them are explained and analysed in this paper.

All the conventional universities in Andhra Pradesh, including Dr. B.R. Ambedkar Open University, are offering the course in Public Administration from undergraduate to the research level leading to B.A., M.A., M.Phil. and Ph.D. degrees. Distance education mode is also very much in demand in Andhra Pradesh and as such all the major universities in the state are offering the Public Administration courses in the distance education mode except Nagarjuna and Sri Krishnadevaraya Universities, not only at the undergraduate level but also at the post-graduate level. The Moulana Azad National Urdu University which was established in 1998 to provide higher educational

Tabe 1 : The students enrolled in Public Administration in A.P. Universities at the Undergraduate Level (2002-2003)

Name of the University	Students enrolled in regular mode (approximate)*
Osmania	7500
Andhra	3000
Sri Venkateshwara	2000
Kakatiya	3533
Nagarjuna	1000
Sri Krishnadevaraya	400
Dr. B.R. Ambedkar Open	
University	---
Moulana Azad National	
Urdu University	---
Indira Gandhi National	
Open University	---
TOTAL	**17433**

* The student's enrollment in A.P.

opportunities to the minority people and to promote the Urdu language is offering Public Administration discipline as one of the co-equal optionals at undergraduate level through distance mode by establishing its study centres.

The figures indicate that Osmania and Kakatiya universities are ahead compared to other universities in terms of the student strength at the undergraduate level in the regular mode. In spite of the disparities existing in the number of total colleges and number of colleges offering this course under various universities, it is quite encouraging that the Public Administration is opted by nearly 18 thousand students in the colleges at the undergraduate level.

The figures pertaining to the distance education mode also are encouraging. The Centre for Distance Education of Andhra University leads, the enrolment strength is 24,000. Dr. B.R. Ambedkar University with a strength of 18,176 closely follows it. Kakatiya University has a strength of 5,491 while the Osmania and the Sri Venkateshwara have modest enrolment of 800 and 260 respectively. The overall intake of students into the Public Administration level in the distance education mode is at least double that of the enrolment in

Table 2 : Students enrolled in Public Administration in A.P. Universities at the Post-graduate Level (2002-2003)

Name of the University	Intake of Students in Regular mode
Osmania	120
Andhra	120
Sri Venkateshwara	60
Kakatiya	55
Nagarjuna	20
Sri Krishnadevaraya	25
Dr. B.R. Ambedkar Open University	---
TOTAL	**400**

the regular mode. Thus, Public Administration appears to be more popular in the distance education system than in the regular system.

Andhra University is leading with a strength of 2,500 students, followed by Dr. B.R. Ambedkar Open University with a strength of 724, Osmania University with a strength of 700 and Kakatiya University with 356. While all the universities in Andhra Pradesh are offering M.A. in Public Administration in the regular and distance modes, in Osmania the regular P.G. Degree is called M.A. in Public Administration and the P.G. Degree in distance mode is called M.A. in Public Personnel Management.

Tabe 3 : University-wise Faculty particulars in Public Administration Programme (Conventional and Distance)

Name of the University	Professors		Associate professors	
	Con.	Dis.	Con.	Dis
Osmania	5	-	3	-
Andhra				
University	3	1	2	-
Sri Venkateswara	4	-	5	-
Kakatiya	6	-	6	1
Nagarjuna	2	-	1	-
Sri Krishna				
Devaraya	2	-	3	-
Dr. B.R.				
Ambedkar Open				
University	-	2	-	1
Total	**22**	**3**	**21**	**2**

Con. – Conventional, Dis. – Distance

Public Administration at the post-graduate level has common syllabus in the First year/ First two semesters along with the Post- graduate course in Political Science, in some universities of Andhra Pradesh. Only in the second year, the syllabus and the course contents differ for P.G. degrees of Political Science and Public Administration in such universities. This pattern is followed both in the regular and the distance education modes in Andhra, Sri Venkateswara and Dr. B.R. Ambedkar Open University.

Taking into consideration the amount of teaching, research and extension activities to be covered by the departments of Public Administration in various universities and their P.G. centers, it can be said that the teachers available are quite insufficient. The inadequate faculty strength of the Public Administration discipline have a definite adverse impact on the quality of teaching Public Administration. There are about 30 Government Degree Colleges and One Junior College, where 31 teachers are working.

How do the students look at Public Administration Education?

The questionnaire served on the undergraduate and post-graduate students tried to probe into the interest of the students in Public Administration education, on availability of the literature and books, quality of the subject and its teaching and the general perception of the students of Public Administration about the future in terms of career prospects etc.

(a) What makes the students study Public Administration?

Fiftyone per cent of the students indicated that they had taken up the subject out of their own interest. Because of the future prospects, Public Administration as an educational subject is capable of attracting students and in fact it is attracting a good number of students to the undergraduate and post-graduate courses. Nintyone per cent of students have a positive attitude towards Public Administration education.

(b) Content and quality of teaching

Fourtythree per cent of the respondents said "it is very good" and 36 per cent, "it is good". Thus, the response that rated it is 'very good' or 'good' put together is above 75 per cent. Similarly, the opinion of the students about the content of Public Administration education is also positive.

(c) Availability of books and literature on Public Administration

The response of the students is, positive. 96 per cent indicated that the libraries of colleges, institutes and universities are well equipped with the literature on the Public Administration both in Telugu and English.

(d) Variety of courses/papers available in Public Administration

The response of the students in this matter is quite mixed and lacked enthusiasm on their part about the various courses available in the Public Administration discipline. There are different reasons for this kind of attitude on the part of the students in this matter. One reason is that most of the colleges do not have adequate teaching staff in the departments of Public Administration and as such they do not offer more optional courses in Public Administration discipline. Secondly, students choose their optional courses blindly following their friends or seniors, without trying to enquire about the courses or papers available in a particular discipline. Another reason that induces the students to opt for one or two courses is their notions about certain papers / courses being "very scoring".

(e) Public Administration Education in Competitive Examinations

Those who rated Public Administration as very good subject for competitive examinations constitute 43 per cent.

Besides 36 per cent of them have rated it as good and 16 per cent of them have termed it as 'average'. Thus total 95 per cent of the respondents in the survey have expressed positive opinion about the usefulness of Public Administration as an optional for competitive examinations. This shows the popularity of Public Administration as a convenient optional for the aspirants of competitive examinations. A general option gathered among the aspirants of competitive examinations has revealed that most of the candidates coming from technical and science backgrounds and even those coming from other social science disciplines background have opted for Public Administration for various competitive examinations, particularly for civil services Examinations and Group-I service examinations.

(f) Students' perception of Public Administration's future

Fiftyone per cent of the students expressed that Public Administration has a good future; 24 per cent of them have termed it as 'very good' and the remaining 27 per cent of them have rated it as 'good'. The total positive opinion about the future of the Public Administration as a discipline constitutes 90 per cent of the total opinions.

As the future of the Public Administration Education is definitely linked with the future of the students studying the subject, a question was included in this survey whether the respondent is interested in pursuing the study of Public Administration further or not. Interestingly 73 per cent of the respondents of undergraduates have expressed their wish to continue the study of Public Administration at the post-graduate and research levels.

Perception of the Teachers on the Status of Public Administration Education

In order to assess the status of Public Administration education as pursued by the teachers of Public Administration, a survey was conducted on this topic among the university and college teachers pertaining to this discipline throughout the state of Andhra Pradesh. Though the response was not very enthusiastic, reasonably good number of teachers respondent to the questionnaires.

Table 4 : University-wise Distribution of Teachers

University	Per Respcoy
Osmania	
Andhra	
Sri Venkateshwara	
Kakatiya	
Nagarjuna	
Sri Krishna Devaraya	
TOTAL	

(a) How many are happy as Teachers of Public Administration?

If the teachers are happy teaching Public Administration then, the discipline can be considered to be enjoying a good status. An overwhelming majority of the teachers, i.e. 86 per cent of teachers expressed happiness being teachers of Public Administration. Those who expressed their dissatisfaction cited lack of interest on the part of the students to join the Public Administration courses at the higher level.

(b) Perceptions on the academic status of the discipline

About the syllabi of different courses offered by the colleges and different universities in the state, the teachers were asked to express their satisfaction or otherwise on the contents of the syllabi. Here the majority of the teachers (57 per cent) expressed their dissatisfaction. The remaining 43 per cent expressed their approval or satisfaction on the contents of the present syllabi pertaining to different courses.

The reasons cited by the teachers for their dissatisfaction on the syllabi : some teachers felt that the Public Administration courses should be professionalised. A few felt that the present syllabus of the subject lacks practical approach. Some suggested inclusion of the following topics in the present syllabi pertaining to various courses of Public Administration at the university and college levels:

1. Leadership Management.
2. Management of Rural Development.
3. Environmental Studies.
4. Office Management with Computer Applications.
5. Administration of Information Technology.
6. Human Resource Management.

The teachers also made the following suggestions, to improve the quality of content of the present syllabi:

1. Inclusion of Project report at the degree level.
2. Synchronise the syllabi with those of competitive examinations.
3. Syllabi should be civil services oriented.
4. Public Administration courses should be professionalised.
5. Practical training must be imparted.
6. Technical know-how should be introduced.
7. Interaction sessions with administrators should be introduced.
8. Students must be involved in consultancy service.
9. Case studies must be introduced.
10. Employment opportunities should be provided.

Status of Public Administration discipline in relation to other disciplines

Fourtyfour per cent of the respondents expressed that Public Administration enjoyed equal status with other subjects, particularly with other social sciences. Twentyeight per cent of the teachers felt that it enjoyed a good status in relation to other subjects. Another 28 per cent of the respondents felt that it enjoyed a low status in relation to other social sciences.

Those who mentioned that Public Administration enjoyed a low status in relation to other subjects stated the following reasons:

1. Public Administration subject is facing problems due to ongoing process of liberalisation, privatisation and globalisation throughout the world.
2. Coping up with the computerisation.
3. Subordination to Political Science. (Only in Osmania and Kakatiya Universities it has good and independent status).

Future of the Discipline

The opinions of the teachers were evenly distributed. Thirtysix per cent of the teachers felt that it has an encouraging future in the coming years and another 36 per cent felt that its future is discouraging. The remaining 28 per cent felt that it has an average future.

On Refurbishing the Image of the Discipline

The teachers were requested to give suggestions to refurbish the image of the discipline. The following suggestions were given by them in this regard:

1. Creating more employment opportunities to the students who obtain the degrees in Public Administration.
2. Updating the existing syllabi of Public Administration courses.
3. Introducing inter-disciplinary approach to the subject.
4. Making the subject market oriented.
5. Publishing the list of candidates who selected to Civil

Services with Public Administration as one of their optionals.

6. Covering all the areas in Public Administration Research.
7. Making Public Administration Courses as professional.
8. Introducing the subject at undergraduate level with new combinations.
9. Making Indian Institute of Public Administration and Indian Council for Social Science Research to concentrate on the development of discipline.
10. Changing the present education system.
11. Improving the quality of teaching at all levels.
12. Selecting talented teachers to teach the subject.
13. Making Public Administration discipline as one of the compulsory subjects to all the existing courses in Higher Education.
14. Introducing the subject at 10+2 level.
15. Involving the faculty of Public Administration in imparting training to the selected civil servants.
16. Publishing textbooks in the discipline in regional languages.
17. Organizing refresher courses in Public Administration to update knowledge of the existing teachers.
18. Strengthening the professional associations.
19. Making the Government to utilise the services of Public Administration teachers.
20. Creating independent departments of Public Administration in all the universities.

Introducing New Papers in the Public Administration programes

The teachers suggested the following new papers to be introduced in the Public Administration programmes:

1. International Public Administration.
2. Administrative Law.
3. Public Service Management.
4. Methods of Management.
5. Human Resource Management.
6. Human Resource Development.
7. Administrative Reforms.
8. International Finance Organisations.
9. Office Records Management.
10. Public Policy.
11. International Economic Administration.
12. Political Economy.
13. Politics of Administration.

Conclusion

The overall impressions gathered from the survey reveal a mixed picture, there is a tendency to blame somebody else for the weaknesses of the discipline. There is a general feeling of dissatisfaction about external factors while the teachers did not show any inclination for introspection or strong resolve to put in more efforts in strengthening the discipline.

Public Administration as an academic discipline enjoyed a reasonably good acceptability and was attracting a good number of students to the undergraduate and post-graduate courses. About the quality and content of the subject as well as the quality of teaching an overwhelming majority of the students at this level have expressed their positive response. Students have also expressed their satisfaction over the status of Public Administration as a subject for the competitive examinations.

A large number of research scholars opined that existing teachers were not properly informed and equipped in intellectual terms. Some scholars have termed the existing teachers of Public Administration in the universities and colleges as 'incompetent, inefficient, dogmatic, ignorant, orthodox and unsuitable'.

A majority of teachers' felt that changes have to be made to the existing syllabi of Public Administration courses at all levels. Some have come out with topics of new areas to be included in the syllabi. The teachers, a majority of them, are also not happy with the kind of research that is being done at present in Public Administration discipline.

The overall outcome of the survey reveal that the status of Public Administration as an academic discipline in Andhra Pradesh in the perceptions of the undergraduate and post-graduate students was very good. The teachers of Public Administration, on the other hand, advocated several suggestions to refurbish the image of the discipline.

10

RESEARCH IN PUBLIC ADMINISTRATION IN A.P.

A. Vijay Kumar

Research is the chief ingredient of knowledge and theory development in any discipline. The split between theory and practice is not new and there has always been a desire to develop a general body of knowledge about Public administration. These two problems are long pending in the research of Public Administration. A modest attempt is made to assess the status, strengths and weaknesses of research in Public Administration in the universities of Andhra Pradesh based on the doctoral work "Public Administration Education in A.P.*

Public Administration as an academic discipline has earned a permanent place in the universities and colleges of Andhra Pradesh state. It is being taught at the undergraduate level in the colleges throughout Andhra Pradesh and at the post-graduate level in all the universities of the state. Many scholars are engaged in research also in this discipline in the universities.

The opinions of the research scholars, are obtained through a structured questionnaire administered on 100 research scholars of all the universities of the state. The

*For details, A. Vijay Kumar, Public Administration Education, Prajahita Prachuranalu, Warangal, 2009.

opinions of the research scholars are recorded, explained and analysed in this paper.

The paper is divided in to three parts: Part one deals with particulars of students enrolled for the M.Phil and Ph.D programmes in Public Administration in the universities of Andhra Pradesh, contents of Public Administration Education at research level, particulars of M.Phil. & Ph.D. degrees

Table 1

University-wise Particulars of M.Phils / Ph.Ds awarded (Regular & Distance mode) (Upto 2003)

Name of the University and Distance Education centre	No. of M.Phil's Awarded		No. of PhD's Awarded	
	Regular	Distance	Regular	Distance
Osmania	83	No Course	100	No Course
Andhra	70	No Course	60	No Course
Sri Venkateshwara	69	No Course	56	No Course
Nagarjuna	15	No Course	11	No Course
Kakatiya	61	6	50	NIl
Sri Krishnadevaraya	35	No Course	21	No Course
Dr.B.R.Ambedkar Open	---	75*	---	31*
TOTAL	333	85	298	37

*Ph.D. in Development Studies is offered. This figure includes commerce and all social sciences. Public Administration is one of them.

awarded by various universities and areas selected by them for the research. Part two deals with the perceptions of research scholars over the problems and prospects of research in public administration and part three deals with the general observations made by the research scholars.

M. Phil.s and Ph.D.s awarded in Public Administration

The following table contains the particulars of M.Phil. & Ph.D. degrees awarded by various universities in the state both in the regular and distance education mode.

Table 1 reveals that various universities in the state have awarded several hundreds of M.Phil, and Ph.D. degrees in Public Administration. It indicates that a lot of research work has gone into this subject, both to promote it among the scholars and also to strengthen it academically. It also augurs well for the subject, in that it has so far acquired such a good number of worthy teachers or prospective teachers in Public Administration.

While it is encouraging to look at the number of research degrees awarded in this subject, it is also necessary to assess the contribution made to the discipline by the research work that has been done so far. It is also important to see whether the research has touched upon all the major areas or aspects of the subject.

PART-I : Perceptions of M.Phil and Ph.D. Scholars

The main issues and questions covered by the survey are:

(a) Reasons for doing research in the discipline.

(b) Topics covered by the scholars in research in Public Administration.

(c) Cooperation extended by the research institutions.

(d) Availability of employment opportunities.

(e) Development of research in Public Administration.

(f) Development of Public Administration education in general.

(g) Popularity of the discipline in competitive examinations.

(h) Future plans of research scholars.

(i) Status of the discipline.

(a) Why the scholars selected Public Administration discipline for research?

The scholars were asked as to why they selected Public Administration discipline for research. Eighty per cent of the respondents expressed that they have taken up research in Public Administration out of their own interest.

(b) Topics of areas covered by the Research Scholars

Majority of the scholars seem to have settled on topics related to three broad areas of the subject, namely.

(i) Panchayati raj and Rural Development Administration.

(ii) Welfare and Development Administration. iii) Health and Educational Administration.

Each of the above areas has covered twenty per cent of the research done by the scholars under the survey. The remaining forty percent of the scholars selected topics related to :

(i) Studies on women.

(ii) Police, Law and Order Administration.

(iii) Environmental and Forest Administration. And

(iv) Problems faced by the research scholars of Public Administration.

It is clear from the selection of topics for research is confined to very few areas of study. Topics on Policy studies, problems related to implementation, analytical studies on various departments of government, studies on theoretical matters etc., are conveniently left out.

(c) Co-operation extended by the institutions to the researchers

TABLE – 3
Opinion of Researchers on the Cooperation extended by the Institutions.

Category of Response	Per cent of respondents
Very Good	10
Good	20
Average	20
Not Good	20
Nil	30
TOTAL	**100**

Most scholars seem to be unhappy because of lack of adequate cooperation from the organisations and institutions concerned. Less than one-third of the scholars expressed that cooperation extended to them by the different organisations is either good or very good. Only 10 per cent of the scholars expressed that they have received very good cooperation where as 20 per cent of them said they received good cooperation from various organisations and institutions they have approached in course of their research work.

Twenty per cent expressed that the cooperation extended to them was just average. The total of good, very good and average categories put together amounts to 50 per cent. Among the remaining 50 per cent, 20 per cent scholars said that the cooperation received was not good and 30 per cent have said that they did not receive any cooperation.

This shows that the research scholars of Public Administration find themselves in an unenviable situation. Because, the organisations or institutions approached by the scholars do not extend the required cooperation in providing information pertaining to their research. This is indicative of the fact that the general social and political ambience does not appear to be conducive for the researchers in general and for those of Public Administration in particular.

(d) Opinions on Employment Opportunities available

The status of any discipline or profession can be termed as healthy or otherwise only on the basis of the employment opportunities available to the persons involved in it. Similarly, the status of Public Administration in Andhra Pradesh can be understood by the perception of the research scholars about the employment opportunities available to them.

The research scholars of Public Administration have a very pessimistic view about the job opportunities available to them. None has expressed that he or she had very good or good employment opportunities awaiting him after completion of the research. Only 20 per cent of the respondents have said that the opportunities available to them are just average. Fifty per cent of the research scholars expressed that they had very less job opportunities whereas the remaining 30 per cent expressed that there were no job opportunities after completion of their research.

PART - II : WHAT DO THE RESEARCH SCHOLARS WANT :

(A) To improve employment opportunities

Most of the research scholars opined that the government should fill up all the vacant teaching positions related to Public Administration in Government junior, degree colleges and universities. Some have suggested that Public Administration subject should be introduced at the intermediate level throughout the state. Some opined that in the government offices where the official positions require the knowledge of Public Administration, such positions should be filled up with the persons who are qualified in the subject. Some even went to the extent of demanding special quota for the students of Public Administration in all the government jobs.

The research scholars opined that in the senior administrative positions in the government and the public sector undertakings, preference should be given to the candidates with an educational background of social sciences in general and Public Administration in particular.

A few scholars suggested that the government institutions and universities should take up research projects so that employment opportunities could be provided to the scholars of Public Administration. Some have also suggested that the government should encourage the scholars by providing such projects to them independently.

(B) For the development of research in Public Administration:

Majority of the scholars felt that all the research scholars of Public Administration should be provided with financial support by the government or universities or other government agencies.

The scholars expressed the need to make arrangements to provide all the requisite information in one specialised library for the research in the Public Administration discipline. It is also expressed that more logistic support should be extended to the scholars by the universities, non-governmental organisations and the government.

Some scholars underlined the need for good working relationship between the supervisor and the research scholar. Specifically, it is felt that the supervisors should devote more time for guiding the research scholars.

A few scholars felt that regional language should be promoted as the medium of research. They felt that conducting of National Educational Test/State Level Eligibility Tests should not be restricted to English medium only. They also opined that institutions like The Indian Institute of Public Administration, ICSSR and the UGC should come forward to provide more fellowships and other financial support to the scholars of Public Administration.

(C) For the development of Public Administration education in general:

Generally, it is felt that provision of more job opportunities to the persons qualified in Public Administration would naturally promote the growth of Public Administration education. Hence it is felt that Public Administration should be introduced as compulsory subject at the 10+2 level. It is also suggested that this subject should be introduced in all the degree colleges throughout the state. All government servants who have to deal with the matters related to the public should be made to undergo a special course in Public Administration. Some scholars have even suggested that qualifications in the subject of Public Administration should be made mandatory for all administrative posts both in the government / public sector and private sector.

Some scholars suggested to reorient the syllabus of Public Administration taking into consideration the changes in the socio economic fields. It is also suggested that the literature on the Public Administration subject should be made available in the regional language.

To improve the quality of teaching and research, conducting of seminars, symposia, conferences, workshops and refresher courses should be held more frequently.

(D) Why Public Administration is a Popular Subject in Competitive Exams?

Several reasons were attributed by the scholars for the popularity of Public Administration in competitive examinations.

1. The syllabus of Public Administration in the competitive examination is limited and easy for the candidates to prepare for the exam.
2. Public Administration is an easily understandable subject.
3. The literature on Public Administration discipline is

easily available in the market as it is being offered in almost all the universities in regular as well as distance mode.

4. Many teachers of Public Administration discipline working either in the degree colleges or in the universities are easily available to the students. It is very easy to receive their guidance or counseling or help or advise etc., to prepare for the competitive examinations.
5. It is possible to score more percentage of marks in the subject.
6. It is no doubt on interesting subject.

(E) The future plans of research scholars of Public Administration:

Interestingly, most of the scholars either wanted to become teachers of Public Administration or 'good administrators' in future. Nearly 50 per cent of the respondents declared that they would like to become administrators in their careers. Slightly less than 50 per cent have expressed their interest in taking up a teaching career (Public Administration). Some of them have shown their preference for the career in civil services but in case of their failure to join the civil services, they expressed their willingness to take up teaching of Public Administration.

PART-III : STATUS OF PUBLIC ADMINISTRATION IN A.P.

Generally, more than half of the scholars sounded pessimistic about the future of Public Administration education in Andhra Pradesh. More than half of the scholars have attributed this to the lack of job opportunities in the teaching profession both in the government colleges and in the private colleges. While in the government colleges the vacant posts of Public Administration are not filled up and in most of the private colleges the "discipline of Public Administration" is being not offered. The scholars felt that on both the counts, the government has to take appropriate decision and implement them.

Some scholars felt that the government is giving step-motherly treatment towards social sciences in general and Public Administration in particular. They felt that if social sciences are not given proper encouragement and support by the government and other private institutions, there is a chance of gradual moral degradation of the society. On the other hand, they felt that by encouraging the discipline of Public Administration, the government could create more job opportunities to the scholars of Public Administration and also ensure the growth of an efficient and effective breed of administrators in the state.

Some scholars have turned their attention towards the quality of the teachers and the contents of the syllabus in Public Administration discipline The general feeling is that the syllabus is out-dated and it needs to be revamped thoroughly. Similarly, very serious negative opinions were expressed by a few scholars about the teachers of Public Administration. The terms used for the teachers of Public Administration are–unsuitable, orthodox, ignorant, dogmatic and inefficient.

Thus, the above mentioned details of the survey conducted among research scholars of Public Administration on the status of Public Administration in Andhra Pradesh reveals a set of mixed opinions. A very positive aspect, which has come out of this survey, is that the research scholars are very seriously interested in the promotion of Public Administration education and its research at the higher education level. They have generally tried to point out the lack of job opportunities, lack of facilities for the serious research, lack of good teachers and lack of proper encouragement by the government. But they have not expressed any lack of interest on their own part. Moreover, at least 50 per cent of the scholars evinced interest in prosecuting a career in teaching Public Administration. All these can be taken as a good omen for the future of Public Administration in Andhra Pradesh.

Other observations made

A close observation of research activities going on in various universities throughout the nation including Andhra Pradesh reveals a few basic problems affecting the academic environment, inter alia, in the discipline of Public Administration. It is these basic problems, which account for the stereotype research-work being done. Some of these problems are:

1. Generally, favouritisms, nepotism and extraneous factors are gaining upper hand over the academic merit in the university departments.
2. Research topics are chosen or allotted not on the basis of the aptitude of the researcher but from the point of view of convenience of the scholar.
3. Duplicity in the selection of the topics with minor variations is a rule rather than exception.
4. Research is being done just for the sake of degrees and in some cases as a means for promotions in the jobs.
5. In most of the cases the thesis is not the original work of the candidate. It is generally a hotchpotch work put together by copying from different sources.
6. There is a serious lack of interest on the part of the supervisor, for different reasons, to make the scholar work sincerely on the thesis.
7. In a number of cases the thesis is written either by the supervisor himself or by some other "ghost writer".

In spite of all the drawbacks mentioned above, research work has made a significant contribution in strengthening the knowledge base of the subject and also in making an impartial evaluation of various policies and projects implemented by the Governments of Andhra Pradesh and India.

11

THEORETICAL PREMISES OF DEMOCRATIC, DECENTRALISED GOVERNANCE AND THE 74TH CONSTITUTION AMENDMENT ACT, 1992 : SOME DEVIATIONS

S.M. Rahmatullah

Introduction

The 74th Constitution Amendment Act, 1992 has accorded the constitutional status of the third tier of government to the Urban Local Bodies (ULBs) and thus acquired to be a subject of several debates and discussions for the last many years. It has been applauded as a significant Act in the history of local governments in India for a number of reasons. It is an undeniable fact that any act or action will prove to be fruitful, if it is based on a well evolved theory. The Amendment Act has been enacted to strengthen the democratic decentralisation in India and came into force on 1st June, 1993 as the "Nagarpalika Act". The question that arise at this juncture is whether the Amendment Act has been enacted on the basis of a well evolved theory of democratic decentralised governance? The intention here is to examine this issue with a view to continue the discourse on the Amendment Act so as to pave the way for further reforms to strengthen the democratic decentralised governance in Urban India.

Significance of Decentralised Governance

The inadequacies of centralised governances concentration of social, economic and political powers in one segment of people, has provided theoretical foundations for the decentralisation of governance. Decentralisation has in recent times received almost universal acclaim as a method of devolution of powers to bring about political stability (World's Development Report 1999, 2000). Brian Smith(1985) in his authoritative work on decentralisation has written that in the Third world "decentralisation has been regarded as a necessary condition of economic, social and political development".

The significance of decentralised governance has been felt because of a number of reasons. It has been found to be a more effective way to meet the local needs, deliver basic public services, dispose work, penetrate the local areas and link up them with the nation as whole, articulate local demands meaningfully, and facilitate local planning and development with the help of local resources, enable local masses to participate in politics and facilitate people's participation in administration and development. Decentralisation has, therefore, been recognised as a means of harnessing public power and civil society's collective energy for sustainable development.

Strong advocacy of decentralised governance has on a number of grounds generated powerful theoretical base in favour of local governments. If democracy in Parliament and State Legislatures is to remain strong and stable, its roots must reach villages, towns and cities where the people live. The acceptance of this theoretical indoctrination has led to the constitution of the institutions of democratic decentralisation, both rural and urban, in India. But democratic decentralisation has been very narrowly operationalised in India restricting its scope to the creation of local bodies and not concentrating, in its true sense, on distribution of powers, functions and resources at various levels of governance.

Theoretical Features of Democratic Decentralisation:

Effective democratic decentralisation requires a fairly well evolved theory of democratic decentralisation. For, a system emerged on the basis of a good theory would certainly serve the purpose. It is, therefore, tried to identify the premises of a theory of democratic decentralised governance and see whether the Amendment Act has been enacted on the lines of such a theory.

It is said that any theory of democratic decentralised governance should possess the following political, institutional, functional and fiscal features.

Political Features

1. Promotion of democracy at the grass root level
2. Compulsory constitution and reconstitution of local bodies within a stipulated frame, thus ensuring continuity of local representatives;
3. Provision for representation in local bodies by certain social, political and ethnic groups who matter significantly in terms of national goals but could not otherwise have a significant role to play in decision-making.
4. Sufficient power to play in the decisive role institutions of self-government.
5. Non-interference of higher level governments in local affairs

Institutional Features

1. Requisite institutional capability to administer civic plans and programmes
2. Improved local administration in terms of effectiveness in dealing with local problems and responsiveness in the redressal of public grievencess
3. Sufficient autonomy and accountability in managing local affairs

4. Development of a sound system of personnel management in local bodies
5. Scope for private partnership in the provision of public services for better performance

Funtional Features

1. Assignment of important functional responsibilities
2. Identification of number of relevant activities within each function for better output
3. Avoiding overlapping of functions of local bodies with other providers of public services in the local area
4. Better matching of the public services of local bodies with the preferences of residents in local area
5. Provision for feedback on discharge of functions by local bodies

Fiscal Features

1. Sufficient fiscal autonomy
2. Provision for mobilisation of local resources
3. Timely transfer of funds from higher level governments on standard lines
4. Provision for mobilisation of finances from market forces
5. Matching of finances with functional responsibilities

The features, thus listed, are generally regarded to be the core elements of a sound theory of democratic decentralised governance.

In the light of above features, it is proposed now to examine whether the Amendment Act has been evolved in conformity with the theoretical premises of democratic decentralised governance to justify whether it has been flaunted to ensure, in true spirit, democratic decentralisation in urban India.

Urban local bodies have got much more important place in the daily life of the urbanites than the State or the Central

Government. For, these are the most closest, accessible and amenable governments to them and the functions these bodies perform are related to the provision of civic amenities to the population within their jurisdictions. If these services are ceased, the urbanites will relapse into chaos. So the urban local governments are of primary importance to the people. But the ULBs have been facing a number of challenges: Scarcity of financial resources, badly drafted municipal laws, substandard personnel and personnel management, unplanned urbanisation, ineffective political leadership, structural lacunae, little coordination between the civic body and civil society, employees organisations and private sector, poor inter-governmental relations, concentration of political parties on higher echelons of power neglecting the local bodies, corruption of every form and stringent state control etc., have been the problems of ULBs.

Further, though the respective Municipal Acts of the States have provided for regular elections to Municipal Bodies, they were frequently suspended and superceded for indefinite periods of time. These trends have eroded the very basis of local self-government and had a negative effect on democracy at the grass root level. Having regard to these inadequacies, the Amendment Act has been enacted to strengthen ULBs. The important features of the Amendment Act are:

- constitutional status to urban local bodies
- Amendment or replacement of State Municipal Laws in force in States by the State Legislatures in conformity with the provisions of the Amendment Act
- constitution of Nagar Panchayats for transitional areas, Municiapal Councils for smaller urban areas and Municipal Corporations for larger urban areas
- fixed five year tenure for the ULBs and regular conduct of elections
- reservation of seats for SCs, STs and Women

- devolution of greater functional responsibilities and financial powers to ULBs
- constitution of Wards Committees in ULBs of cities to facilitate larger participation in urban governance
- constitution of State Finance Commission to review the financial position of the ULBs and make recommendations to strengthen them
- constitution of State Election Commission for the superintendence, direction and control of the prepatation of electoral rolls and the conduct of elections to ULBs
- constitution of District Planning Committee to prepare a draft of district development plan for the district as a whole; and
- constitution of Metropolitan Planning Committee to prepare a draft of metropolitan development plan for the metropolitan area as a whole, etc.

But it is a fact that the Amendment Act has not provided much scope for a few core aspects of the democratic decentralised governance. Functional and fiscal empowerment and provision for the involvement of NGOs in the delivery of public services for better performance have been lagged behind. In the absence of these aspects of democratic decentralised governance, mere political protection of the ULBs through the Amendment Act does make neglizible sense. For, these bodies can play effective and efficient role in self-rule and local development only if they possess all the features of democratic decentralisation. It is relevant to mention here a few pitfalls of the Amendment Act that come in the way of democratic decentralised governance.

Empowerment of ULBs through functional devolution is an important objective of the Amendment Act. It has added a new Twelfth Schedule to the Constitution containing 18 important functional items that may be assigned to ULBs by the States. These are:

1. Urban Planning including town planning.
2. Regulation of land use and construction of buildings.
3. Planning for economic and social development.
4. Roads and buildings.
5. Water supply for domestic, industrial and commercial purposes.
6. Public health, sanitation, conservancy and solid waste management.
7. Fire services.
8. Urban forestry, protection of environment and promotion of ecological aspects.
9. Safeguarding the interests of weaker sections of society, including the handicapped and mentally retarded.
10. Slum improvement and up-gradation.
11. Urban poverty alleviation.
12. Provision of urban amenities and facilities such as parks, gardens and playgrounds.
13. Promotion of cultural, educational and aesthetic aspects.
14. Burials and burial grounds, cremation grounds and electric crematoria.
15. Cattle pounds, prevention of cruelty to animals.
16. Vital statistics, including registration of births and deaths.
17. Public amenities including street lighting, parking lots, bus-stops and public conveniences.
18. Regulation of slaughter houses and tanneries.

Pitfalls

Let the objective of the Amendment Act be so strong and ambitious in identifying the functional responsibilities for ULBs, but much depends upon its actual implementation.

An overall experience, in this regard, is that on the plea of one or the other reason, the States have not adopted fully, in true sense, the provision of the Amendment Act concerning to the devolution of functions to the ULBs. In most of the States though the 18 functions have been included in the list of municipal functions, the transfer of functions have taken place only on paper. In a few other States, the ULBs have remained superficial without required functional responsibilities. Why this has happened? The crux of the problem is that the Amendment Act does not make it mandatory for the State Governments to devolve compulsorily all the functions to the ULBs. Consequently, the States have got much scope to make use of this ambiguity in the Act and assign functional responsibilities to the local bodies according to their whims and fancies. What is required urgently is that a re-thinking is to be made in the concerned provision of the Amendment Act to ensure devolution of functional responsibilities to ULBs in conformity with the theory of democratic decentralised governance.

Sufficient fiscal autonomy and financial self sufficiency is a prerequisite for democratic decentralisation. The Amendment Act, has envisaged that every State is required to constitute a State Finance Commission, every five years, to review the financial position of Municipalities and to make recommendations to the Governor as to the :

(i) Distribution between the State Government and Municipalities of the net proceeds of the taxes, duties, tolls and fees leviable by the State.

(ii) Determination of the taxes, duties, tolls and fees which may be assigned to or appropriated by the Municipalities.

(iii) Grant-in-aid that would be given to the Municipalities from the Consolidated Fund of the State.

(iv) Measures needed to improve the financial position of the Municipalities.

(v) Any other matter referred to the Finance Commission by the Governor in the interest of sound finances of the Municipalities.

The actions taken by the state authorities on the recommendations of State Finance Commissions have been documented in the action taken reports of the States. A review of the reports reveals that contrary to the expectations of the Amendment Act, no considerable improvement in the financial position of the ULBs has been witnessed since the passage of the Amendment Act. The main reason for this pitiable position is that though the major thrust of the Amendment Act is on strengthening the financial condition of Municipalities, it has also not been made mandatory for the States to accept the recommendations of the State Finance Commissions. Whatever may be the intention of the framers of the Amendment Act in tailoring it in this way, the lacuna of this kind in the Amendment Act has provided much liberty to the States to control the strings of the purpose of the ULBs. Under this circumstance, can it be claimed that the Amendment Act has paved the way for democratic decentralisation, in its true sense, in India? In order to overcome the deficiency, measures to ensure the implementation of the recommendations of State Finance Commissions are, in true spiritrequired to be undertaken.

Major transformations are taking place in the role of the State and the philosophy of governance all over the world. Participation of the community and the private sector, specially in the delivery of public services, is being emphasised as an important factor of decentralisation now-a-days. According to Public Choice Theorists, market forces can be tapped to acquire adequate financial support and to provide competition and consumer choice in the provision of public services. But, it is also unfortunate that the Amendment Act does not encourage the institutions of local governance for facilitating private sector participation in urban infrastructure. For the efficient performance of the functions of ULBs, mentioned in the Twelfth Schedule of the Constitution, private sector could be involved. This would, certainly, enable the ULBs to enhance their image. A provision to facilitate the partnership of NGOs with the assurance of some sort of morality in the delivery of civic services to meet the growing demand for these services in urban areas is required to be inserted in the Amendment Act. It will certainly pave the way for democratic decentralisation and for the improved performance of ULBs.

The lack of clarity in the Amendment Act about the functional responsibilities and financial powers and in the institutional flexibility of the ULBs needed to be provided in the context of Liberalisation, Privatisation and Globalisation, do come in the way of democratic decentralisation and leave these bodies in a state of shambles.

CONCLUSION

In a nut-shell, the 74th Constitution Amendment Act, 1992 has accorded constitutional status, prescribed uniform structure, ensured representation of the weaker. sections of the society through reservations and larger sections of the society through wards committees and provided political protection to the ULBs. But it is true that it has not been guided by a well evolved theory of democratic decentralised governance, as it has done little for the empowerment of municipal bodies in terms of functions, finances and the transformations taking place in the role of State and philosophy of governance all over the world so as to enable them to function as the true institutions of democratic decentralisation.

References

1. Arora R (ed). People-Centered Governance, Jaipur, Rawat Publications, 2001.
2. Brian Smith. Decentralisation: The Territorial Dimension of States, London, George Alien and Unwin, 1985.

3. Constitutional Provisions Relating to Village Panchayats and Municipalities in India containing Text of the Constitution (Seventy-Third Amendment) Act, 1992 and the Constitution (Seventy-Fourth Amendment) Act, 1992 Lucknow, Eastern Book company, 1992.
4. Hoshiar Singh. "Conceptual and Theoretical premises of 74th Constitution Amendment Act and Public Private Partnership", Nagarlok, New Delhi, I.I.P.A. Vol. XXXI, No. 1 January-March 1999.
5. Hussain M.A. Urban Governance and Politics: A Case Study of Tirupati, The Indian Journal of Political Science, Vol.LXVIII, No.3, July-September, 2007.
6. Jain R.B. Public Administration in India: 21st Century Challenges for Good Governance, New Delhi, Deep and Deep, 2001.
7. Mishra S.N., & Sweta Mishra. Decentralised Governance: Macro and Micro Perspectives, Delhi, Shipra Publications, 2002.
8. National Foundation for India (NFI), Accountability and Decentralisation in Urban Governance, Report from the workshop held on October, 1994, New Delhi.
9. Paramita Majumdar. "Decentralisation : Challenges to Urban Local Governments", Nagarlok, New Delhi, J.I.P.A., Vol. XXX VIII, No. 3, July-September, 2006.
10. Prasad. Public-Private-Partnership in Urban Infrastructure, KERALA CALLING (February 2004).
11. Sofi Ali. Urban Governance in India - Issues and Challenges, Keynote address, 9th Conference of the New Public Administration Society of India, Kakatiya University, Warangal, A.P., 27th January, 2007.
12. World's Development Report, 1999, 2000.

12

RIGHT TO INFORMATION ACT-2005

T.V. Sujatha Kumari

Right to information has necessarily been the key to strengthening participatory democracy, empower the poor and the weaker sections of society to demand and get information about public policies and actions, thereby leading to their welfare. Without good governance, no amount of developmental schemes can bring improvements in the quality of life of the citizens. Good governance has four elements—transparency, accountability, predictability and participation. Transparency refers to availability of information to the general public and clarity about functioning of governmental institutions. Right to information open up government's records to public scrutiny, thereby arming citizens with a vital tool to inform them about what the government does and how effectively, thus making the government more accountable. Transparency in government organisations makes them function more objectively there by enhancing predictability. Information about functioning of government also enables citizens to participate in the governance process effectively. In a fundamental sense, right to information is a basic necessity of good governance.

In recognition of the need for transparency in public affairs, the Indian Parliament enacted the Right to

Information (RTI) Act in 2005. It is a path breaking legislation empowering people and promoting transparency. While right to information is implicitly guaranteed by the Constitution, the Act sets out the practical regime for citizens to secure access to information on all matters of governance. In the words of Prime Minister : "Institutions to be effective they must function in a transparent, responsible and accountable manner. The right to information bill will bring into force another right which will empower the citizen in this regard and ensure that our institutions and the functionaries discharge their duties in the desired manner. It will bring into effect a critical right for enforcing other rights and fill a vital gap in a citizen's framework of rights".

Purpose of the ACT

As per the preamble of the Act the aim is :

> To provide the citizens right to information which will enable them to have access to information under the control of the public authorities which will promote transparency and accountability in the working of every public authority.
>
> To provide for the constitution of a Central Information Commission and State Information Commissions.

The Act will extend to the whole of India except the State of Jammu and Kashmir. The Act gives every citizen of India a Right to Information.

Meaning of Information

Information has been defined as "any material in any form, including records, documents, memos, email, opinion, advices, press releases, circulars, order, logbooks, contracts, reports, papers, samples, models, data material held in any electronic form and information relating to any private body which can be accessed by a public authority under any other law for the time being in force".

Definition of Right to Information

Right to information under the Act means as the right accessible under this Act, which is held by or under the control of any public authority and includes the right to:

(1) inspection of the work, documents, records;

(2) taking notes, extracts or certified copies of documents or records;

(3) taking certified samples of material;

(4) obtaining information in the form of diskettes, floppies, tapes, video cassettes or in any other electronic mode or through printouts where such information is stored in a computer or any other device.

Authorities Under the Act

For providing information it has been made incumbent on every public authority to designate within a period of 100 days of the enactment of this Act, Central Public Information Officers or State Public Information Officers as the case may be, in all its administrative wings for the purpose of providing information to the person so requesting and central Assistant Public Information Officer or a State Assistant Information Officer at each sub-divisional level or other sub-district Public Information Officer or State Information Officer or Central Information Commission or State Information Commission as the case may be.

Procedure for Supply of Information

A person who desires to obtain information has to make a request for the same in writing or through electronic form. It can be in English, Hindi or in the official language of the area in which the application is being made. Such application shall be accompanied with the prescribed fee. The application is to be made to the Central Public Information Officer or State Public Information Officer of the concerned public authority or Central Assistant Public Information Officer or State Assistant Public Information Officer as the case may be. The particulars of the information required must be specified in the application. No areas or personal details are required to be given for seeking information. The application must either be decided within a period of 30 days or the request be rejected for the reasons as specified under the Act.

Restrictios on Right to Information

The information under the Act be denied if–

Disclosure prejudicially effects sovereignty and integrity of India, security, strategic, scientific or economic interests of the state, relation with the foreign state or lead to incitement of an offence:

- Publication of the information is expressly forbidden by court of law or tribunal and disclosure constitute contempt of court.
- Information disclosure of which, causes breach of privilege of the Parliament or the State Legislature.
- Information includes commercial confidence, trade secrets or intellectual property and disclosure would harm competent position of the third party unless the competent authority is satisfied that the public interest warrants disclosure of such information.
- Information available to the person in his fiduciary relationship unless the competent authority is satisfied that larger public interest requires disclosure of such information.
- Information received in confidence from the foreign government.
- Information whose disclosure endangers the life or physical safety of any person or identifies the source or assistance given in confidence for enforcement of law or security purposes.
- Information which would impede the process of investigation or apprehension or prosecution of offenders.

- Cabinet papers including records of deliberations of the Council of Ministers, Secretaries and other officers. However, the decisions of the Council of Ministers and the reasons and material on which the decisions were taken shall be made public after the decision has been taken provided it is not covered under any of the exemption clauses mentioned.
- Personal information which has no correlation to any public activity or interest or which causes unwarranted invasion of the privacy of the individual unless larger public interest justifies the disclosure of such information.
- Providing information involves an infringement of copyright subsisting in a person other than state.

Central and State Information Commission

The Act provides for creation of the Central Information Commission and State Information Commission at Central and State levels. The Central Government shall constitute Central Information Commission consisting of Chief Information Commissioner and Central Information Commissioner not exceeding 10 in number. They should be appointed by President on recommendation of committee consisting of Prime Minister as Chairperson, Leader of Opposition and Union Cabinet Minister nominated by the Prime Minister. The Chief Information Commissioner(CIC) and Information Commissioners (ICS) shall be person of eminence in public life with wide knowledge and experience in law, science and technology, social science, management, journalism, mass media or administration and governance. CIC shall hold office for a term of five years or till he attains the age of 65 years which ever is earlier and shall not be eligible for reappointment. IC shall also have a term of five years or till he attains the age of 65 years which ever is earlier. IC shall also not be eligible for reappointment as IC but he may be considered as CIC provided his term of office on appointment, as CIC shall not be more than five years in aggregate as IC and the CIC. Salaries and allowances and terms and conditions of the CIC shall be the same as that of a Chief Election Commissioner and the 1C as that an Election Commissioner. CIC and IC can be removed from office by the order of the President on ground of proved misbehavior or incapacity. This can be done after an inquiry made by the Supreme Court on a reference made by the President.

Similarly, every state government shall constitute State Information Commission, which shall consist of State Chief Information Commissioner and State Information Commissioners not exceeding 10 in number. The appointment shall be made by the governor of the state on the recommendation of the committee consisting of the Chief Minister who shall be the Chairperson of the committee. Leader of the Opposition in the legislative assembly and a Cabinet Minister to be nominated by the Chief Minister. The State Chief Information Commissioner (SCIC) and state Information Commissioner(SIC) shall be person of eminence in public life, with wide knowledge and experience in law, science and technology, social science, management, journalism, mass media or administration and governance. SCIC shall hold office for a term of five years or till he attains the age of 65 years whichever is earlier and not eligible for reappointment. SIC shall also have a term of five years or till he attains the age of 65 years whichever is earlier. SIC shall also not be eligible for reappointment as SIC but he may be considered as SCIC provided his term of office on appointment, as SCIC shall not be more than five years in aggregate as SIC and the SCIC. Salaries and allowances and terms and conditions of the SCIC shall be the same as that of an Election Commissioner and the SIC as that of the Chief Secretary of the State government. SCIC and SIC can be removed from office by the order of governor on ground of proved misbehavior or incapacity. This can be done after on inquiry made by the Supreme Court on the reference made, by the governor.

The duty of the Central Information Commission and State Information Commission involves—

1. To receive and inquire into a complaint from any person:
   - (i) Who has been unable to submit a request to Central Public Information Officer or State Public Information Officer because of
     - non appointment of such officer or
     - refusal of Central Assistant Public Information Officer or State Public Information Officer to accept the application or appeal to be forwarded further
   - (ii) Who has been denied access to the information requested; (iii) Who has not been given response to request within time limit specified.
   - (iv) Who was required to pay unreasonable amount of fee.
   - (v) Who believes information provided is incomplete, misleading or false.
   - (vi) Any other matter relating to request or access of information.

(2) Initiating inquire into any matter if Commission is satisfied that there are reasonable grounds to inquire into the matter.

APPEAL; The Act provides for two stages of appeals. At the first stage, the appeal lies against the decision of the Central Public Information Officer or State Public Information Officer. If the person does not receive a decision within the time specified or aggrieved by the decision of the Central Public Information Officer then within 30 days from the expiry of such period or from the date of receipt of the decision, prefer an appeal to officer who is senior in rank to the concerned Public Information Officer (PIO).

When first appeal is made by the concerned third party against the order of the concerned PIO in respect of the disclosure of the third party information it shall be done within 30 days from the date of order.

A second appeal lies against the decision of the appellate authority in the first appeal to the Central Information Commission or the State Information Commission. The appeal shall be preferred within 90 days from the date on which the decision should have been made or was actually received.

PENALTY

If the Central Information Commission or the State-Information Commission at the time of deciding a complaint or appeal is of the opinion that the Central Public Information Officer or the State Public Information Officer has

- without any reasonable cause refused to receive application for information or has not furnished information within time specified under Section 7 (1) or
- malafidely denied request for information or
- knowingly gives incorrect information, incomplete or misleading information or
- destroyed information which was subject of request or
- obstructed in any manner in furnishing information.

It shall impose a penalty of Rs 250 each day till application. Further it shall recommend for disciplinary action against the Central or State Information Officers as the case may be under the service rules applicable to him/her.

SCOPE

The Act covers the whole of India except Jammu and Kashmir.

It is applicable to all constitutional authorities, including the executive, legislature and judiciary; any institution or body established or constituted by an Act of Parliament or state constituted by order or notification of appropriate government including bodies "owned, controlled or substantially financed directly or indirectly by funds" provided by the government are also covered in the Act's ambit.

Private bodies are not within the Act's ambit directly. However, information that can be accessed under any other law enforce by a public authority can also be requested for in a landmark decision of 30-Nov-2006 (Sarbajit Roy versus DERC) the central information commission also reaffirmed that privatised public utility companies continue to be within the RTA Act – their privatisation not withstanding. The Act and other laws enforce 15-June-2005 to the extent of any inconsistency.

Essential to ensure the Right to Information Act Successful

1. **Education and Training in the Art and SCIENCE of records keeping:** Right to information can be successful only if the government at all levels maintain information (Records) seriously. It is generally seen that the information is generally patchy. When a citizen wants some information, it becomes difficult to send him a correct report. There is a need to infuse consciousness of the art and science of records management and its proper follow up.
2. **Awareness to people through Public Relations about to Information Act.** The creation of awareness is integral to social and economic development. The possibility for the power of communication to liberate the minds and potential of people to critical awareness is real in every field linked to human development and the generation of public willingness on effective communication of information and ideas that relate to people's needs, aspirations and capacities for progress in the thought of information, education and communication through public relations.

3. **Need of Transparency at all Levels :** Transparency of governance and right to information should be fundamental rights of all people. These are the basic guarantees for human and social developmenf" said K.R. Venugopal. To protect the above right, government decisions need not be clouded in secrecy, except in the interest of national security. Based on the discussion of an Inter-Ministerial Working Group, a statutory scheme to ensure freedom of information subject to certain safeguards and to amend a number of central legislations, has been formulated. State Governments could undertake a similar legal exercise, while endorsing the central initiative and ensure greater openness in the working of the Government departments, public agencies and elected local bodies and provide information on procedure for various statutory approvals.
4. **Need of Empowering People through Information of Right Time and Place :** To quote A.B.Vajpayee, Former Prime Minister of India, information about many developmental schemes, be they of the Centre or the States, does not always reach the common people, especially in rural and remote areas. When people have no information, they can hardly participate in their implementation or monitor their progress. In the absence of people's participation, such programs are invariably implemented in the usual bureaucratic manner. This breeds corruption, inefficiency and lack of accountability. As a result, common people become cynical about governmental programs and schemes. Often even MPs and MLAs too are not involved in the implementation process. The active participation of the people and of people's elected representatives is a must for the success of all developmental endeavours. The Ministries of Information at the centre and states have a vital role in correcting this imbalance.

5. **Understanding Modern Technology to Provide Information to the citizens at a fast rate** : Modern technology has been able to make a major contribution towards improved management practices, with respect to information systems. The contribution is possible because of two factors—firstly, the generally increased sophistication of management theory and practice, permitting the identification of information needs and uses; and secondly, the developments of electronic data processing, permitting the analysis of huge quantity of data in a short time to permit its use.

6. **Need of Designing code of Ethics for The Public Services to avoid too much Information** : The constitutional and administrative role of the public services is to assist the duly constituted Governments of whatever political colour, in formulating and implementing policies of the Government and in administering the public services under the Central Government in the most effective manner, within the frame work of the Indian Constitution. It is the obligation of every employee in the public services to uphold the Rule of Law and respect for human rights and to act solely in the public interest while making recommendations or exercising administrative authority. He or she must maintain the highest standards of probity and integrity.

   In relation to the general public, employees in the public services should conduct themselves in such a manner that the public feels that the decisions taken or the recommendations made by them are objective and transparent and are not calculated to promote improper gains for the political party in power, for themselves or for any third party.

7. **Obligation to Government and the Constitution:** Employees in the public services should not seek to frustrate or undermine the policies, decisions and

actions taken in the public interest by a duly constituted Government by declining or abstaining from action which flows from ministerial decision or statutory obligations where, following the instruction of the superior authority, implementation of such decisions or action would appear to conflict with the exercise of impartial professional judgement, or affect the efficient administration of the department or undertaking, the employees should set out the points of disagreement clearly and courteously writing to the superior authority and seek explicit written instruction thereon.

8. **Accountability and Responsiveness to the Public**: Public Accountability is a facet of administrative efficiency. Consistent with accountability to the superior officers and the Ministers in accordance with Constitutional provisions, employees in the public services should be accessible to the people and practice accountability to them in terms of quality of service, timeliness, courtesy, people-orientation and readiness to encourage participation of and form partnerships with citizen groups for responsive government.

   Employees in the public services should be consistent, equitable and honest in their treatment of the members of the public, with particular care for the weaker section of society and should not appear to be unfair or discriminatory decisions in pursuit of discretionary powers should be. justifiable on the basis of non-arbitrary and objective criteria. Employees in the public services should accept the obligation, recognise and enforce the citizen's right for sppedy redressal of grievances and commit themselves to provide service of declared quality and standards to citizens. Employees in public services should respect the right of the public to Information and enforce the citizens and transactions except where they are debarred from releasing information by provisions of law or valid instructions.

The ultimate purpose of all these reforms would be to setup spiritual or enlightened organisation.

9. Utility of Information Generated through RTI Act, 2005 for Future Improvements : Right to Information consciousness at the Union and State levels should not provide only information but should also analyse this information with the help of a research cell to –

(a) Understand the status of Government machinery

(b) Understand the factors which stand in the way of development

(c) Understand the problems and difficulties faced by the people affected by Government policies.

(d) Understand the working of Government Schemes aimed at the welfare of the people

(e) To understand the bottlenecks in the way of development

(f) To understand the levels of corruption.

(g) To suggest remedies to avoid recurrence.

In this way, the Right to Information would help in promoting good governance.

10. Encourage People Participation in Development Activities through Sharing Information with the People : Development is a multi-dimensional phenomenon, which cannot be achieved, unless the community itself is involved. Resources available with any Government are limited, especially in the developing countries like India. Communities, according to their capacity, need to mobilise human, financial and material resources to supplement their sources provided by the national Government and other extra-community sources, in order to effectively carry out local improvement efforts. Substantial financial and human resources can be mobilised from the community, some of which may otherwise remain unused, such as the enthusiasm and energy of youth and women for community action, communities with institutional structures, such as local government, a cooperative society or a community which have a degree of control over the community development programmes more easily than those relying on voluntary and individual contribution. Thus, the community participation is most widely seen as a way to mobilise resources for that would otherwise not be available. A Government promoting to meet the diverse needs of the people may be faced with expenditure, it could not meet the needs if the entire effort had not to be financed out of the public purse. So, in order to cut costs, the intended beneficiaries themselves contribute for the extension of community activities.

Community participation involves members of communities in planning, implementing and monitoring of activities. Thus, community is wholly involved in the programme, rather than being asked to either contribute or take advantage of the services offered under it. Community participation is the process in which individual, families assume responsibility for their own programme. They come to know their own situation better and are motivated to solve their common problems. This enables them to become agents of their own development, instead of being passive beneficiaries of development aid, They, therefore, need to realize that they are not obliged to accept conventional solutions that are not suitable. They have to acquire the capacity to appraise a situation, weigh the various possibilities and estimate what their own contribution can be.

CONCLUSION

The Right to Information law of 2005 signals a radical shift in our governance culture and permanently impacts all agencies of state. The effective implementation of this law depends on three fundamental shifts: from the prevailing culture of secrecy to a new culture of openness: from personalised despotism to authority coupled with accountability: and from unilateral decision-making to participative governance. Obviously one single law cannot change everything. But this fine legislation is an important beginning. Its effective application depends largely on the institutions created, traditions and practices, attendant changes in laws and procedures, and adequate participation of people and the public servants. The Commission, therefore, focused on two broad categories of issues.

The first set of issues relates to changes in other laws and practices involving state secrets, civil service conduct rules and classification of documents. The Commission firmly believes that the Official Secrets Act, 1923 in the current form is antiquated and unsuitable to emerging needs. The second set of issues relates to implementation of the RTI Act itself, in particular process engineering, record keeping, disclosures, access and monitoring. In respect of the second category of issues, the Commission's recommendations are largely within the framework of the law.

It is well recognised that the right to information is necessary, but not sufficient, to improve governance. A lot more needs to be done to usher in accountability in governance, including protection of whistle blowers, decentralisation of power and fusion of authority with accountability at all levels. Nevertheless, this law provides us a priceless opportunity to redesign the processes of governance, particularly at the grass roots level where the citizen's interface is maximum. Now that the romance of the struggle for transparency is over, the tedious process of system-building has to take over. It is in this spirit that the Commission made specific recommendations and attempted to provide a road map for their time-bound implementation.

References

1. Government of India, Second Administrative Reforms Commission, First Report on Right to Information, 2006.

2. Goel S.L. Right to Information and Good Governance, Deep & Deep Publications, NewDelhi, 2007.

3. Jayatilak Guha Roy. Second Administrative Reforms Commission on Right to Information; A Critical Review, The *Indian Journal of Public Administration*, Vol. LIII, No.3, 2007.

4. Mahendra Kumar Seth and Baman Panda. Perspectives on India's Right to Information Bill, *Social Change*, Vol. 35, No. 1, March 2005.

5. Sapna Chadah. Right to Information Regime in India : A Critical Appraisal, *I.J.P.A.*, Vol. LII, No. 1, 2006.

13

GLOBALISATION AND THE LABOUR MOVEMENT : SOME NOTES*

V. Bhaskara Rao

"Globalisation" refers to the widening and deepening of the international flows of trade, capital, technology and information with in a single integrated global market. Globalisation involves the liberalisation of national and global markets in the belief that the flows of trade, capital and information will produce the best outcome for growth and human welfare (UNDP 1992). Globalisation is a consciously pursued strategy, the political project of a transnational capitalist class and formed on the basis of an institutional structure set up to serve and advance the interests of capitalist class. This class is formed on the basis of a complex of some 37,000 transnational corporations (TNCS), the operating units of global capitalism. Apart from these TNCS the World Bank, International Monetary Found and Other International Financial Institutions constitute "the Global Financial Net Work". Including some other international institutions form an integral part of the new system of "global governance" and the "World Capitalist System".

* This note is based on James Petras and Henry Veltmeyer, Globalisation Unmasked: Imperialism in the 21st Century, Madhyam Books, Delhi, 2001.

Labour under Globalisation

The brunt of globalisation process has been borne by labour, the restructuring of which in effect has been the major mechanism of Structural Adjustment Programme (SAP). In the 1980s and 1990s capital launched a direct assault on labour in terms of its wage, conditions and benefits, as well as labour's capacity to organise and negotiate contracts. In the global context it is estimated by UNCTAD (Third World Guide 95/96 : 28) that up to 120 million workers are now officially unemployed and another 700 million are seriously under - employed, separated from their means of production and eking out a bare existence accounting for over 50 per cent of the developing world's labour force (I LO 1996). In addition to this surplus labour, it is estimated that a mobile labour force of 80 million expatriate labourers formed to constitute a new world labour market.

The structural adjustment process has separated large numbers of direct producers from their means of production, converting them into a proletariat and creating a labour force which at the global level was estimated to encompass 1.9 billion workers and employees in 1980, 2.3 billion in 1990 and about 3 billion by 1995 (ILO 1996). Moreover, the demand for labour has grown more slowly than its supply. It has generated an enormous and growing pool of surplus labour estimated at one-third of the total global labour force.

The Adversaries and Exploited Classes

The major adversaries of globalisation have been the peasant movements in Latin America, Asia and Africa. Free trade policies have led to the devastation of local producers, unable to compete with cheap grain imports. Subsidies to agro-export producers have stimulated the concentration of land ownership, credits and technical assistance at the expense of small producers. It witnessed a growing mass of radicalised peasants and landless rural workers in Latin American countries and India.

Workers in France, Germany. South Korea, Brazil, Argentina, South Africa and many other countries have engaged in general strikes against globalisation policies. In the developed countries, workers protested strikes have been mounted against threats of plant relocations, cuts in pensions, health plans and vacations and the massive growth of job insecurity. In the developing countries workers have mobilised against low wages, despotic working conditions, autocratic managerial rule, long workdays and declining social benefits.

Another class of adversaries is the bulk of public employees affected by budget privatisation and massive loss of purchasing power. The opposition of this class is found in all the countries of the world. While the advocates of globalisation have their own international forums and organisation and act in common, the exploited adversaries remain fragmented. While the advocates and beneficiaries of globalisation (Ex: Agro-business, financial groups, importers. mineral exports, big manufacturers for export markets) could weld their capacity to control the nation-state for creating conditions for global expansion, the weakness of adversaries is in part organisational opposition is built around sectorial demands without strong international ties and ideological commitments. Adversaries have been sidetracked from the struggle for state power by the rhetoric of "Civil Society" and the notion that "the nation-state is an anachronism".

While the capitalists have taken hold of the state, labour remains a pressure group, an outsider, linked to sectorial struggles and narrow wage issues. While capitalists dominate the mass media, labour lacks any alternative media, while capitalists launch wave after wave of anti-labour legislation, intensifying the class struggle from above, labour turns towards service activities as its members decrease.

Perspectives of Globalisation

Globalisation as an economic strategy was the consequence of an ideological project backed by state power and the "national unfolding" of the market. Since the globalisation has a strong ideological component, it is important to confront it in ideological terms. The hard fact is – great majority of nations and the immense majority of humanity are opposed to current globalisation in practice, if not in thought.

In reality, the social conditions to day are in fact reverting to those of the 19th century. Health care all over the world is more precarious and more dependant on income levels. Job insecurity is on the increase. Impoverished families are forced to work at below subsistence. More workers work longer hours to-day. Retirement age is nearly reaching 70 years old. Employers no longer provide pension plans. Inequalities surpass 19th century levels. The future for the young generation looks insecure and fearful.

Dynamics of Globalisation

The "big push towards globalisation" was a result of a dramatic change in the political power away from leftist, populist, and nationalist regimes towards globalist governments. In social terms, the "big-push" resulted from the defeat and retreat of trade unions, and the declining influence of the working class, lower middle class and peasantry.

The greatest social crisis is the number of workers without medical coverage, non-unionised workers, temporary or part-time workers with little or no social benefits in the U.S.A and U.K. and unemployment rates in the third world are increasing.

The concentration of power in the hands of employers at the expense of wage workers leads to unilaterally fix terms for hiring, firing, outsourcing, sub-contracting and other means of increasing the rate of exploitation, lowering labour costs.

The fact of the globalisation is that the capitalist class every where to a large extent defeated the working class in every sphere of life: "In state control, social policy and ideology; at the factory level in work rules, wages, bargaing power and employment; and at the personal level in vulnerability, conscious and fear".

Since the early 1970s, the capitalist class has taken advantage of a highly bureaucratised trade union movement divorced from the rank and file and highly dependent on state favours to roll back labours bargaining power. While capitalist class developed close ties with the political parties of the state and thus wield effective power over their politicians, the labour bureaucratic leaders have continued to depend on essentially the same capitalist parties to further their interests. While capitalists have developed a forthright and coherent strategy that bars concessions on welfare issues, labour bureaucrats have remained tied to the concept of social contracts and the welfare state and have been unable and unwilling to develop an anti-capitalist strategy or consider a socialist alternative.

Working class defeats throughout in the 1970s and the collapse of the USSR and the conversion of social democrats to neoliberals and U.S. Liberals to free-market conservatives were the political events that transformed state policy from a force mediating between globalisation and supporting international flows of capital and commodity trade.

Globalisation has provoked a serious social crisis affecting wage workers, peasants, employees and the self-employed throughout the world. Globalisation policies have engendered a significant increase in inequality between the minority and those who exploited by it. Taxes have become increasingly regressive. The salaried and wage groups have been paying more taxes but their welfare measures have been on decline.

Globalisation and Nation-State

The globalisation ideologues have propagated the notion that the nation-state is a anachronistic or weak before the onslaught of globalizing corporations. But the reality is otherwise: The nation- state has never played a more decesive role or intervened with more vigour and consequence in shaping economic exchanges and investment at the local, national and international levels. The multinational corporations would not have expanded without approval of the leaders of the nation-sate in politics, military and economic experts. The nation-state silently supported the plans and programs of the globalists. The scale and scope of nation-state activity have grown to such a point that it is referred to as "New Statism" rather than free market. Therefore, Globalisation may be considered at the first instance as a product of the new statism and continues to be accompanied and sustained by direct state intervention.

Thus, the centerpiece of globalisation is the overarching political frame work, i.e the role of the state in eliminating the welfare state diminishing regulations on overseas flows and demolishing political and economic constraints in overseas markets. The political-economic role of the state is accompanied by the deep penetration of the police, military and intelligence of the dominant nations like U.S.A.

The nation-states which are dubbed as weak serve to disarm the critics of globalists, discouraged oppositional social forces from creating an alternative to globalisation. The globalists, through the nation-state disoriented the political struggle, encouraged political and social groups to operate in the interests of the dominant system. The purpose is to create dependent links with globalist classes. The great majority of NGOS, "Civil Society" actors and the apex of the state have multiplicity of links.

Despite the dynamic and central role of the nation-state in the globalisation, we must identify the tremendous potentials of the state as a centre for alternative forms of economic organisation. These could be public sector enterprises, self-managed cooperatives and decentralised planning in the reallocation and redistribution of income, credit, land and technical assistance.

The neoliberal policies of globalisation have profound consequences for democracy and society. Substantive citizenship is in profound conflict with the coercive practices of TNCS citizenship can only function when citizens can elect decision makers while not under the influence of external actors. The role of citizens as protagonists of public policy debates has declined. The result is greater voter apathy, increased abstention, rejection of political incumbents, "anti-voting" and increased resort to extra parliamentary action.

Resistance to Globalisation

1. While electoral vehicles have been one source of opposition, extra-parliamentary action has been the most wide spread and effective approach to blocking or limiting the application of globalist policies.
2. All the groups adversely affected by globalisation have turned towards extra-parliamentary activity and organisation: General strikes, land occupations, urban revolts, guerrilla movements etc. These movements defend rights and interests threatened by the globalist ruling classes. Some of the movements have taken the offensive and sought to advance towards structural changes the peasant movements, the landless workers movements, revolutionary armed forces.
3. All movements in opposition to globalism is the tendency to form coalition with environmental, gender, ethnic groups and struggles.

Alternatives to Globalisation

The critics of globalisation repeatedly felt the need to create an alternative rejecting the existing i.e the free market and the bureaucratic statism. A few have begun to examine the real world and the emerging alternatives created by militants and activists. The alternatives of today are found in the local projects insurgent groups and in the programmatic transformation of movements in struggle. Some forms of Alternatives emerging are:

(a) Brazilian rural cooperatives network which includes 1.50.000 families

(b) Self-governing Indian Communities under Zapatista Leadership in Chiapas

(c) Municipal enterprises organised in China

(d) Socialist-led regional rural producers in Colombia and Bolivia

(e) Proposals to democratise universities in Chile and Argentina

(f) Self-management proposals set forth by the radical wing of trade unions in France, South Korea and Italy.

All these are parts of a larger political project of social transformation. They are initiated by insurgent groups in confrontation within the globalist state and classes and they are internally democratic. These alternatives are born of struggles that increase class and national consciousness and point towards the creation of an anti-globalist bloc based on democratic collectivist alternatives. These alternatives struggle for a social economy, which combines sustainable growth, entrepreneurship and economic democracy. In the search for alternatives to globalisation involves a profound rethinking of the comparative advantages of privatilation and socialisation in historic perspective. It is clear that socialisation is for more working people, the waged, salaried and self-employed for greater job security, wider health coverage and more access to public higher education. Socialisation provides an alternative democratic model in which capital becomes social capital and it will be subordinated to the new generation of state power and decentralisation of authority to the committees of different works. Socialisation redistributes wealth and reorients production and media to serve democratically chosen social values. It is called as "post-globalist socialism" built on democratic and internationalist principles.

Realisation of Some Facts

If the adversaries of globalisation do not want free market and bureaucratic statism, then what is their choice? They desire a new socialist society, the new nation as an integral whole, a new culture of participants and not spectators, and a new internationalism of equals. However, the construction of a new socialist society require a long and hard struggle, the concerted collective action of the most diverse groups in society and the mobilisation of their forces of opposition and resistance.

14

POLITICAL CORRUPTION IN INDIA : COALITION DHARMA?*

K. Tummala Krishna

INTRODUCTION

Political corruption may take many a form, the worst of which is to use, or misuse, the Constitution for political and partisan purposes, confusing or substituting party interests to that of a nation (Tummala 2006: 1-22). Then there is the perennial issue of gerrymandering by which the party in power re-writes the boundaries of constituencies in such a way to give it a polling advantage which does not occur in India as delimitation of the constituencies is given to a statutory body. There is the continuous flow of money, legal and illegal into party coffers from rich individuals and political action committees (PACs) thus buying access to power points and influence policy preferences. The 2009 budget in India proposes that contributions made to political party trusts would be tax-deductible one hundred percent. However, a certain transparency and accountability are available in these transactions since the 2003 amendment to the 1950 Representation of Peoples Act[1]. Moving from one party to another in search of wanted positions continues to be a problem despite the 1985 Anti-defection Law which would

* Revised Version of the Paper Published in International Public Management Review, Vol. 11, Issue 2, 2010.

disqualify any legislator who switches party affiliation but would allow a third of a party members to change parties in mid-stream. But the most pernicious problem of political corruption occurred during the 2008 confidence motion in Parliament, and events leading to the 2009 general elections, where legislators were bought and sold like chattel while cobbling majorities in a coalition government.

If politics were to be the art of the possible, everything possible was artfully unleashed in India in 2008. It was not free market politics, but a bazar barter that happened as the Congress party-led United Progressive Alliance (UPA) coalition government of Prime Minister Manmohan Singh won a confidence motion on July 22, 2008. It was Indian democracy at its nadir, and political corruption at its zenith. If a stable and mature democracy like India could indulge in shoddy political behavior, what might less stable or unstable democracies do? And how to prevent this kind of behaviour? In other words, what is the coalition dharma[2] the right conduct of the various constituents of a coalition? Analysing and discussing the fortunes of the Singh coalition government, this article is organised under several headings. The first starts with a few introductory remarks. The second analyses the 2004 general elections leading to the UPA coalition. The third explains the 2008 politics and the consequences of the no-confidence test. The final section concludes by summing up the situation and offering some suggestions.

In a parliamentary form where there are only two prominent parties, as was the case in Britain for long, the majority party formed the government, while the other party sat as the "loyal opposition", waiting to take its turn. In times of emergencies, there however have been instances when national unity governments were formed with several parties participating in the governance of a country. But that is only an exception. Yet, over time, due to the growth of multi-party systems, parliamentary forms did turn to coalition governments. Also, in electoral systems following Proportional Representation (PR) where each party would have its members elected proportionate to its voting strength, coalition governments are also a norm. Here a coalition government is defined as one where no party gets the majority to form a government, and several parties come together to form a majority government. This could be due to three factors: the coalition partners may be like- minded, more or less; it could be just opportunism to share power; or it could even be to prevent the other group of parties from coming into office. In any case, the Prime Minister is dependent upon the support of the several coalition constituents for his / her survival in power'.

India does not have PR, but has a multi-party system with a first-past-post electoral system. Even when the Congress Party was dominant, it could not muster absolute majorities in Parliament, but did form stable governments. However, since the late 1960s as the Congress party declined while several regional parties grew in several States, coalition governments have come to be the norm. The Centre had its first coalition put together by the Janata Party following the defeat of the Congress government of Indira Gandhi in 1977 further to the national emergency she declared (Tummala 1998: 497-510; 2002a: 43).

THE 2004 GENERAL ELECTIONS AND THE UPA COALITION

The National Democratic Alliance (NDA) government of 1998 at the Centre, which was put together by Prime Minister Atal Bihari Vajpayee of the BJP was the first in a long time to serve the normal five year term. Starting with nearly 25 different parties, this coalition ended up with 18 when the Prime Minister called for new elections in 2004. He was buoyed by his own party's "feel good" factor and the perceived decline of the Congress Party. But as it turned out, his optimism was ill-conceived. BJP succeeded in winning 138 seats (of the 545 members in the lower House of Parliament-the Lok Sabha) while Congress garnered 145 seats (Tummala, 2004a: 31-58).

For a successful formation of any coalition, it is important to find out the relative policy positions of each of the parties so that like-minded parties may come together. The election manifesto of the Congress (2004) party declared that this election did not mean a simple choice between two parties (themselves and the BJP, the other main contender), but “a clash of sharply competing values, of diametrically opposite ideologies”. Criticizing the BJP that it contributed nothing to the Freedom Movement leading to India’s independence in 1947, and opposing its credo of Hindutva (Hindu nationalism), the Congress declared that its own goal “is to defeat the forces of obscurantism and bigotry...whose sole objective is to subvert our millennial heritage and composite nationhood”. Thus, it put itself up as a bulwark of secularism, as opposed to BJP’s Hindu nationalism.

The BJP/NDA government was criticised for its several failures: increased unemployment; lowered economic growth; distress to farmers and farm labourers leading to several suicides; weak national security due to paucity of expenditure; damaged social harmony through acts such as riots in Gujarat, encouragement of allegedly communal and fascist groups such as Vishwa Hindu Parishad (VHP) and Bajrang Dal (who have been part of BJP), and so on. It was also held responsible for subverting school curricula in favor of Hinduism and spreading hatred of others; encouraging corruption; denigrating key institutions such as the Central Vigilance Commission (CVC), the Central Bureau of Investigation (CBI); and undermining foreign policy by not speaking forcefully against the marginalisation of the United Nations and flip-flopping on the relations with Pakistan.

The Congress party instead promised to: promote social cohesion and harmony; ensure to each family a viable livelihood; improve income and welfare of farmers and labourers in all the villages; unleash the energies of entrepreneurs and the middle class; empower women; and provide equal opportunity to all the backward classes and other religious and linguistic minorities.

Efforts would also be made to improve the public distribution system (PDS) of food, focusing primarily on those who fall below the poverty line (BPL). The Panchayati Raj scheme started by former Prime Minister Rajiv Gandhi launched by the 73rd and 74th Amendments (to the Constitution) of 1992, would be strengthened by the devolution of functions and funds to local governments (Tummala 1997: 49-64).

However, once the need to form a coalition government was obvious, Congress could not rest on its own party manifesto, but needed a platform which would be more or less acceptable to the nineteen parties willing to join hands. Thus came the Common Minimum Program (CMP) (2004). Congress took pride in its electoral victory, and in writing the CMP acknowledged thus: "The people of India have voted decisively in the 14th Lok Sabha election for secular, progressive forces, for parties wedded to the welfare of farmers, agricultural labour, weavers and weaker sections of society, for parties irrevocably committed to the daily well-being of the common man across the country."

Reminding that the CMP is a minimum starting point reflecting its priorities, the UPA government proclaimed six basic principles of governance: (i) Reflective of its indictment of BJP for its supposed Hindu fundamentalism, it promised to promote and protect social harmony; (ii) Expected to work for the economic growth of 7-8% annually to ensure a viable and safe livelihood to each family; (iii) Would provide for the welfare of farmers and farm labour; (iv) Ensure the empowerment of women; (v) Secure full equality of opportunity, in particular in education and employment, to all dalits, tribals, other backward classes (OBCs) and religious minorities; and (vi) Unleash the energies of all professionals and productive forces.

Realising that the previous government neglected the rural populace, the CMP also emphasised the importance of rural growth. The government hoped to enact a National Employment Guarantee Act to provide to rural households a minimum wage employment in public works for at least 100 days each year. It expected to launch administrative reforms to revamp public administration, promote E-governance, and a more meaningful right to information. It looked toward ensuring the welfare of workers, particularly the 93% of work force which constitutes the unorganised labour sector. Reflecting the concerns of the Left parties, privatisation of public enterprises would be carried out on a case-by-case, and with the intent of creating competition, and not to create monopolies. The fiscal deficit was expected to be eliminated by FY 2009.

Of the several parties in this coalition, the Communists (the Left) were of particular concern. There are four parties in this group: communist party of India-CPI; Communist party of India - Marxists (henceforward for brevity, (CPM), Revolutionary Socialist party (RSP); and Forward Block. With a combined strength of 61 seats in Parliament, what could, or should be their role ?

The post independence Congress government of Jawaharlal Nehru was cheered on by the Communists at first. But the dismissal of the Kerala State Government in 1957, the first elected communist government anywhere in the world caused friction between the communists and Congress, which was further aggravated by the war between China and India in 1962.

The CPM won 43 seats in parliament. Congress party needed their support. The Communists, as ideological opponents of multi- nationals, want to end the disinvestment of government enterprises something which has been going on since the 1990s. But both Congress and the Left professed secularism. As opponents of BJP's Hindu nationalism, both parties were also happy to see the BJP government out of office. They declared their support to the Congress led government from outside, without being a part of it. Thus came into power the United Progressive Alliance (UPA) led by Congress. Without being a part of government, but offering their support, the Left thus came to eat the cake and have it too in that they began using their power over the UPA government policies, but without responsibility and accountability (Tummala 2007: 139-160).

THE POLITICS OF 2008

The travails of coalition governments are not unknown. In a coalition, parties with disparate ideologies and agendas come into a marriage of convenience. But when one or the other dissatisfied partner withdraws support, the government gets weakened and may even fall. In case of the UPA government, the cause celebre was the nuclear treaty which the Singh government negotiated with the United States. This treaty would allow the US access to and supervision of Indian civilian nuclear facilities. In return, India would be allowed access to nuclear technology and fuel from the US. The Singh government felt the urgency to get this approved by Parliament as President George Bush's term in the US was to come to a close soon. And the Bush Administration itself was exercising its own pressure to get this deal done before they went out of office. But the Opposition in India thought otherwise.

The BJP thought that India stands to lose its sovereignty, and more ominously, the United States would come to exercise control over Indian foreign policy. The Left too shared such fears. Under the circumstances, the Left struck first, declaring that they would withdraw their support to the Singh government. That left Prime Minister Singh and his UPA government vulnerable. The Prime Minister had no alternative but call the bluff of the Left and seek a vote of confidence in his government. It is even claimed by some political pundits that the Congress party was tired of the Left for long, and actually was looking for an excuse to get rid of them from the coalition as they (the Left) kept obstructing economic liberalisation (Chawla 2008: 8). The vote was set for July 22, 2008, preceded by a two-day parliamentary discussion. On the eve of the confidence vote Congress could count the support of 260, while the opposition could muster 263 (including 2 independents). Eighteen were undecided including 4 independents, and with two of the SP members in jail (Aiyar 2008: 13).[3]

Given such fluidity, everyone saw an opportunity, but each faced unique troubles. The first of course was the Left. The second was BJP. Third was an alliance of assorted parties-the so-called Third Front, previously known as UNPA. And the fourth of course is the Congress party. As neither of them could stand alone (the Opposition to bring down the government, and the Congress to continue in office), each began looking for new coalition partners.

(i) The Left, having flexed their political muscle in creating a near political debacle, now had not only the need to continue its influence but also find an alternate government, should the Congress coalition fall. But given their limited strength in Parliament, they could not go alone; they never did. But with whom would they coalcse ?

(ii) The Opposition BJP also objected to the nuclear treaty with the US arguing that future Indian nuclear exercises would be impaired if the new treaty went through. They thought that India's nuclear future capability thus would be hampered, although it is not clear whether indeed there was a clause prohibiting nuclear tests and other developments.

(iii) Given the weak position of the Left as well as BJP, the possibility of the often talked about and the previously dead, third party alliance (UNPA) came alive. By its very nature, this was a motley group led by various leaders from time to time. In this context, led by Chandrababu Naidu (of TDP), it started promoting

Mayawati as its leader and a possible Prime Ministerial candidate. She promptly declared that toppling the UPA government as the sole objective of the Third Front.

(iv) With the loss of support from the Left, and having called for a confidence motion, the Congress-led UPA government had to seek support from whichever party or member of Parliament that could be forthcoming. The first to announce substantial support was SP leader Mulayam Singh Yadav along with the General Secretary of the party, Amar Singh. SP has 39 members in Parliament.

Then there were other minor parties who were willing to negotiate, keeping their eyes on the general elections to be held before May 2009. Of these, Chandrasekhar Rao of TRS first approached the Congress with the suggestion that his 3 MPs would support the UPA government if he was promised a separate Telangana state.

Former Prime Minister Deve Gowda (JD-S), with three members, bargained for a Ministerial berth. He also wanted the support of Congress in his home State Karnataka so that he could topple the incumbent BJP government there. Neither came his way, and he did not support the UPA government. Similarly, Ajit Singh, leader of Rashtriya Lok Dal, with three members in Parliament, was another target for Congress. To appease him, the Congress government in a hurry re-named the Lucknow airport after his father and former Prime Minister, Charan Singh. But he could not be bought.

(v) Among the other intriguing stories was that of the Speaker of Lok Sabha, Somanth Chatterjee. Although elected to Parliament on a party ticket, once elected as Speaker one is expected to be non-partisan in conducting the proceedings of the House. In this case, Chatterjee found himself on a sticky wicket in that he was elected to Parliament as a CPM candidate. Having withdrawn its support to the government, his party demanded that he resign as Speaker, rather than preside over the parliamentary session dealing with the confidence motion. He refused. There was even speculation whether he should not be voting with the government should there be a tie. Mercifully, this did not happen. He did conduct the proceedings with dignity and even indignation. While everyone agreed that the Speaker was exceptionally impartial and conducted the proceedings of the House fairly, within 24 hours of the vote in Parliament the CPM politburo on July 23rd expelled Chatterjee from the party for having defied the party.

Other parties followed by expelling their errant members. SP in its turn expelled six of its MPs as they defied the party whip and did not vote for the UPA government. TDP kicked out one of its members for voting with the UPA government, and sought an explanation from another. The BJP expelled eight of its members for similar reasons.

(vi) Not unexpectedly, a lot of political drama unfolded with numerous charges and countercharges. CPM leader Bardhan alleged that Congress was buying support of members of Parliament paying them exorbitant sums of money. In fact, on the day of voting, BJP allowed three of its members to walk into Parliament with wads of money which they waved claiming that it was a bribe given to them by Amar Singh of SP seeking their vote for the UPA government. A private TV channel claimed that it had secretly taped the transaction and given the tape to the government the day before the vote took place. BJP leader Advani, while denouncing the TV channel for its underhanded workings, nonetheless not only used that information to criticize the government but also demanded an inquiry into the alleged scandal. It is of interest to note that a parliamentary committee later found Amar Singh innocent of the bribery charges. But the Delhi police registered a case, and an investigation is on.

Then there were six other members who were in jail, convicted of several crimes including extortion, kidnapping and murder. They had to obtain special permission from courts to attend the Parliament session and vote. The most notorious of these was a Mohammad Shahabuddin, who won his election to Parliament from the state of Bihar while he was actually sitting in a jail. There were other members, who were allowed to vote from the lobby of the Lok Sabha as they were indisposed. At least one who had heart surgery in Mumbai was flown in to vote.

As scheduled, the confidence vote was taken on July 22, 2008. While 275 of the total effective strength of 541 in the Lok Sabha voted with the government, 256 voted against, with 10 abstentions. While indeed the government survived, the occasion gave rise to low politics at the lowest with several charges of corruption and horse-trading, as seen above. Harish Salve, former Solicitor-General of the Government of India was quoted by Times (London, 2008: 25) saying: "This is the defeat of Indian democracy that we have seen. The spectacle they created was disastrous."

CONCLUSIONS

Before we draw some conclusions, it is of interest to note what has been happening since the confidence vote was taken, and as a prelude to the general elections scheduled for April-May 2009. The first concerns Shibu Soren who landed as the Chief Minister of his State of Jharkhand. As he was not elected to the legislature at the time of assuming the position of Chief Minister, Soren chose to contest an Assembly seat four months later. Normally, a safe constituency is selected. He ran from Tamar where the sitting legislator was gunned down by the Naxalites. And the electorate on January 8, 2008 shot Soren down. This was an unusual experience where a sitting Chief Minister was not elected to the legislature.

Worse, instead of resigning as the Chief Minister as required by the Constitution and also by convention, and despite the calls from Congress leaders among others that he resign. Soren wanted to think through the issue, as if there was one. First he declared that he would contest the election, again. Another legislator in fact resigned thus vacating a constituency to accommodate Soren. Then, he said he would go to New Delhi to consult with UPA leaders. Meanwhile, he also began canvassing the UPA allies that they accept his son, Champai Soren, as the leader of JMM (which was not so covert a way of stating that he be made the Chief Minister). In any case, nearly a week went by before he resigned on January 12, 2009. He continued as a care-taker Chief Minister as tradition goes, till such time a new Chief Minister is chosen. But none came forward to form a new government. Consequently, the Governor sent a report to the Centre stating that there was a failure of constitutional machinery in the State. Based on that, President's rule was declared on the 19th. The 81 member Legislative Assembly whose term expires in March 2010 itself was left in a limbo.

The second incident was about Mayawati. Each year in January her birthday is celebrated with great pomp and circumstance, when huge amounts of money were collected as gifts to her. As usual this year, collections went on. When one of the civil servants, a public works engineer- refused to contribute, he was beaten to death allegedly by one of Mayawati's supporters, a legislator, who is now in jail awaiting trial on murder charges. The family of the murdered engineer, having initially refused assistance from the Mayawati government and demanded a CBI inquiry, soon changed their mind. In return to dropping their demands, they were given (they accepted) a nice bungalow in the Raj Bhavan colony (where senior Indian Administrative Service officers live), a Class II job to his son and other financial perks. This volte face occurred on January 13th-just two days before Mayawati's birthday, leading to charges that the family was bought off, after all. In the meanwhile, the SP

General Secretary, Amar Singh, complained to the Election Commission wherein he claimed that he has evidence (he released a CD) that large sums extorted for Mayawati's birthday were being transferred into small demand drafts to show, wrongly, that they were all small contributions from several of her small-time donors.

Mayawati, previously petitioned seeking that corruption charges against her be dropped saying that they were politically motivated. The CBI claimed that in 2003 whereas her assets were Rs. 10 million, by 2007 she was showing the same as Rs. 500 million. And in July 2008, they told the Supreme Court of India that they have sufficient evidence to prove her assets were disproportionate to her income. On January 12, 2009 the Supreme Court gave four weeks to her to respond to the CBI claim, but nothing is heard so far. (One should note that these charges were levied some five years ago.)

As the general elections are coming closer, the usual and inevitable efforts at alliances are under way. The first such concerns CPM. So far as Karat is concerned, his goal still is to prevent both Congress and BJP from coming to power. CPM and Congress continue to be bitter rivals in both the States of Kerala and West Bengal where they would be facing each other. And their opposition to BJP is already shown. But they started working out electoral arrangements with other parties. At the Central Committee meeting in Kochi. CPM's Sitaram Yechury said: "We have an understanding with the A1ADMK in Tamil Nadu. Telugu Desam Party (TOP) in Andhra Pradesh and Janata Dal (secular) in Karnataka." Yet, there would be no alliance with BSP although they would still consider that part} as a part of non- Congress and non-BJP group. Mayawati for herself announced that her BSP will contest all the 80 Parliament seats from UP on her own although she might reconsider only if the CPM earmarks a few seats for her party in Kerala and West Bengal (Radhakrishnan 2009: 6-7).

Amar Singh of SP, who played the most significant role in bailing out the UPA government, expressed reservations about that government's limited progress and the purported weak response towards Pakistan (since the Mumbai terrorist attacks on November 26, 2008). He even thought that Congress leaders "betrayed" the SP when they allegedly tried to lure four SP members of the State legislature into their fold. For a while, SP's continued support to UPA coalition appeared doubtful. But Mulayam Singh Yadav denied any such eventuality whose own fate was hanging in balance due to a case against him in terms of disproportionate wealth he allegedly accumulated. In fact, once Yadav supported the Congress-UPA government, the CBI has soft-pedaled the case which angered the Supreme Court to the point it accused the CBI of acting as agents of the Congress government. What turns up in this context is imponderable.

BJP had its own troubles. In the first instance, there had been an internal struggle between Advani and Rajanath Singh for the leadership of the party. Bhairan Singh Shekawat, former Vice President of India, too challenged that he shall be considered as Prime Ministerial candidate of BJP because of his seniority and past position. High powered and financially strong industrialists such as Anil Ambani and Sunil Mittal went on record that they would support Narendra Modi as another possible Prime Ministerial candidate of that party. The RSS has been pushing the party to be more pro-Hindu while resurrecting the issue of building Ram Mandir (over the site of the demolished Babri mosque). Advani had to remind everyone that he did not forget that – an issue that lost steam a while ago, though considered useful during the previous elections. Thus only two small parties – Indian National Lok Dal and Asom Gana Parishad – threw their lot with BJP.

Within Congress's "dynastic" politics there has always been the unresolved issue of what Sonia Gandhi's position is as a possible Prime Minister. The meaningless issue of her foreign birth keeps coming up despite the fact she was married to a former Prime Minister (Rajiv Gandhi) for long. But more importantly, her son Rahul Gandhis is being promoted as Prime Ministerial candidate by some Congress leaders. And then, Manmohan Singh underwent open heart surgery in February 2009, thus raising the question whether he would be able to take the burdens of the Prime Minister in future although both Sonia and Rahul Gandhi themselves announced that he would indeed be the head of government.

SUMMATION AND CONCLUSIONS

The above analysis shows that among the several political parties, there are no saints. And political bargaining continues; opportunism abounds. The essential question thus is whether these coalitions are meant to pursue office and thus power, or in pursuit of some policy preference. Indeed, the UPA government led by Congress has been pursuing economic liberalisation, and BJP keeps arguing for Hindutt'a – Hindu nationalism. And the Left, who in a way played the villain with their ideological commitment against the Congress efforts at economic liberalisation, also ardently wish to keep BJP out. Thus, the crucial issue is whether there is an alternative in the form of a Third Front. Given all the varied demands of each of the several constituents, and more importantly, the individual ambitions of the leaders of the several units, this appears to be unrealistic. A coalition cobbled together only with a negative intent of keeping other larger parties (be it Congress or BJP) away from power cannot last long, even if it were possible to form such a coalition. In the CPM Central Committee meeting mentioned above, the Third Front was not even mentioned. Thus, it is obvious that coalition governments are the only possibility which also means bargaining and jockeying for power resulting in "unholy alliances", as had been known, will continue raising the fundamental question: What should be the proper conduct of the coalition constituents?

There is always an inevitable conflict in any coalition which is succinctly put thus by Timmermans and Andeneg

(2000:393): "In coalition systems, a fundamental tension exists between the formulation of joint policies and the preservation of a distinct identity by each of the governing parties." In this context some credit must be given to CPM, given their ideological commitment. Yet, they inflicted upon the UPA government the indignity of not being a part, but only to drive its own agenda with no responsibility, worse no acountability. And the other parties seem to be pushing for being in office for whatever reasons. That is irresponsible and an injustice to the electorate and would guarantee further political corruption.

Being only "in office and not in power," (Cronin 1935: 534) resulting in stalled or under-development of the nation is not something that one would like to see. One might argue what all this fuss is about in that India's economy is doing well with an expected growth of 6-7 percent even in the current world-wide economic meltdown; it is a nuclear power; and an IT powerhouse. The answers are many. India's new found wealth is pretty much restricted only to the urban areas; India's villages remain poor, or even getting poorer. How much more growth could have occurred if somehow corruption is curbed is any one's guess. Finally, economic well-being cannot offset the political mess that is being created and perpetuated. So what could be done to ensure right conduct of the parties?

1. Opportunistic alliances should not be encouraged and not allowed to be formed. More so, when two parties fight each other at State level, but allied together at the Centre. This smacks of nothing but simple opportunism, be it to be in office one way or the other, or keep the other "rascals" out. If they are opposed to each other at one level, there is no logic or sanctity in being allies at another. There is already a common parlance to this kind of arrangement – "unholy alliances". Once the number of small and opportunistic parties is reduced, silly alliances may not even be

necessary.

2. The alliances are abetted further by the thought that "today we might fight, but tomorrow we could be friends". This perpetuates the unworthy alliances.

3. Joining and leaving a coalition willy nilly, not based on any ideological grounds but to suit the needs of the day, must somehow be stopped. When a party joins a coalition, it must be bound by whatever minimum program they agreed to. Thus, a coalition should stand or fall in its entirety.

4. The practice of giving support to a coalition without being a member of the government must be prevented. This is the worst kind of opportunism. If a party successfully pushes for a policy stance, then that party must also take the responsibility for governance and be held accountable. By not being a part of the government, and running a government by stealth is not democracy.

5. Proliferation of parties, however undemocratic it might sound, must be stopped. How many parties are needed for a successful working of a democracy is a debatable issue. But there does not appear to be any reason to have many fragmented, small parties, particularly those with no well defined ideological positions, and not a ghosts's chance of coming to power, and run a government.

Most of the above can be accomplished without touching the Constitution, and only by simple legislative measures such as amending the Peoples Representation Act and empowering the EC. But then this argument assumes that the EC itself insulated from the hurly burly of politics and certainly not brought under the control of the government in power. Again, the burden is thus on the political parties and their leaders.

The need of the hour is a disciplined party system led by honorable and just party leaders who shall abide by the admonition of Mahatma Gandhi not to indulge in one of the seven sins – politics without principle. Otherwise, the adage that "tomorrow is another day" when all things are possible as usual will continue to operate abetting political corruption.

Notes

1 However, it is noted that of Rs. 4 billion (about $80 million) raised by 16 political parties in 2006-07, but sources of raising only Rs. 160 million (about $3.2 million) were disclosed. See the story, "Cleaning It Up," in India Today, July 20, 2009, p. 7.

2. The dictionary meaning of the Sanskrit word dharma variously denotes obligation, justice, charity, ultimate law of all things, and perhaps more appropriately here, right conduct.

3. The 260 UPA supporters were thus: Congress 153; SP 35 (without some rebels, but with two of the rebels); RJD 24; DMK 16; Nationalist Congress Party 11; PMK 6; JMM 5; Lok Janashakti Party 4; Muslim League Kerala 1; Republican Party of India (A) 1; Sikkim Democratic Front 1; National Loktantric Party 1; Bharatiya Navashakti Party 1; People's Democratic Party 1.

   Among the opposition 263: BJP 130; Shiv Sena 12, Biju Lok Dal 11; Janata Dal (United) 8; Shiromani Akali Dal 8; CPM 43; CPI 10; All India Forward Block 3; Revolutionary Socialist Party 3; Bahujan Samaj Party 17; Telugu Desam Party 5; Asom Gana Parishad 2; Kerala Congress 2; Veerendra Kumar JD-S; 1; MDMK 4; (SP rebels) Munawar Hasan and Jai Prakash 2; Independents 2.

   Among the undecided 18: Telengana Rashtra Samithi 3; AIMIM 1; Janata Dal (S) 2; Rashtriya Lok Dal 3; National Conference 2; All India Trinamool Congress 1; Mizo National Front 1; Nagaland People's Front 1; Independents 4.

References

Ahmed, Farzand, and Rahman, Shafi. July 21, 2008. "The M Factor," India Today: 21.

Aiyar, Shankar, July 21, 2008. "It's Deal Time Folks," *India Today*: 13.
Bhattarjya, Satarupa, with Chawla, Prabhu, December 24, 2007.

"Comrade Terminator," in *India Today*: 11.

Chawla, Prabhu, July 21, 2008. "Securing the Future," *India Today*: 8. Chawla, Prabhu, July 28, 2008. "The Day of the Dealmaker," *India Toady*: 8.

Chawla, Prabhu, April 13, 2009. "The Great Prime Minister

Bazaar," *India Today*: 13.

Congress, 2004. Party agenda http://www.congressandesh.eom/manifesto-2004/2.html "National Common Minimum Programme of the Government of India, May 2004" Posted by the Prime Minister's Office, http:// pmindia.nic.in/cmpbody.htm July 2, 2004. Quotes in the text are from this document.

Cronin, A. J., 1935. The Stars Look Down Boston: Little, Brown and Company: 534.

Doron, Gideon, February 6, 2009. BBC News. http://newsvote.bbc.co.uk.mpapps/pagetools India Today, December 24, 2007: 7, and 11; January 13, 2009: 10; July 20, 2009: 7. Manifesto, Congress: http://www.congressandesh.eom/ manifesto-2004/2.html.

Muller, Wolfgang C. and Strom, Kaare, eds. 2000. Coalition Governments in Western Europe Oxford: Oxford University Press: 562.

New York Times, July 18, 2008: 12.

Prime Minister's Office, 2004. "National Common Minimum Programme of the Government of India, May, 2004" http:// pmindia.nic.in/cmpbody.html, July 2.

Radhakrishnan. M.G.. January 26, 2009. "The Great Leap Backward," India Today, 6-7.

Rahman, Shafi. July 21, 2008. "Battle for Numbers: The Left," India Today: 17. Rahman, Shafi, March 2, 2009. "Legislative Death Row," India Today: 8-9. Riordin, William L., 1995. Plunkitt of Tammany Hall New York: Signet Classic, 3.

Sahgal, Priya, July 21, 2008. In "Double Take," quoting Amar Singh saying "I had gone to Sonia's house, there I was insulted and called a beggar and a dog and thrown out." *India Today*: 19.

The Times, London, July 18, 2008: 25.

Timmermans, Arco, and Andeweg, Rudy B., 2000. "The Netherlands: Still the Politics of Accommodation?" in Muller, Wolfgang C. and Strom, Kaare, eds., 2000. Coalition Governments in Western Europe. Oxford: Oxford University Press: 393.

Tummala, Krishna, 1997. "Politics of Decentralisation in India: An Analysis of Recent Developments," *Asian Journal of Political Science* 5, No. 2: 49-64.

Tummala, Krishna, 1998. "India's Experiment with Coalitions: The 1996 Elections and Since," *Asian Profile* 26, 6: 497-510.

Tummala, Krishna, 2002a. "Administrative Reform in India," in Ali Frazmand, ed., Administrative Reform in Developing Nations. West Port, CT: Praeger, 2002 : 43.

Tummala, Krishna, 2002b. "Corruption in India: Control Measures and Consequences," *Asian Journal of Political Science* 10, No. 2 : 43-69.

Tummala, Krishna, 2004a. "The 2004 General Election in India and its Aftermath," *Asian Hournal of Political Science* 12, No. 2 : 31-58.

Tummala, Krishna, 2004b. "Democracy V. Fundamentalism: Religious Politics of the Bharatiya Janata Party in India," in Santosh Saha, ed., Religious Fundamentalism in the Contemporary World: Critical Social and Political Issues Lanham : Lexington Books : 207-234.

Tummala, Krishna, September 2006: "Regime Corruption in India," *Asian Journal of Politcal Science,* 14 : 1-22.

Tummala, Krishna, 2007. "Developments in Indian Federalism: 2005-2007," *Asian Journal of Politcal Science* 15, No. 2 : 139-160.

15

ADMINISTRATION AND ENVIRONMENTAL CONCERNS

Srinibas Pathi

Present day world is sometimes depicted as a bundle of complexities and paradoxes. The human society in general and individuals living in different nation states in particular face a very peculiar situation. Everybody would like to achieve rapid development. But development brings in a number of issues and problems for administration including that of environmental degradation. As a result of such a situation environmental discourse is the thing today. All of us are well aware that either we have a common future or no future. We have used, misused and abused the environment and the natural resources as if these are to continue for an unlimited period of time. It is of course true to a great extent that Nature has enough of resources to fulfill our genuine requirements: but at the same time we have to remember that there is so little with Nature to cater to our unlimited greed. One of the findings says that it takes nearly one hundred years to create natural products like petroleum oil and gas which we can consume within less than a year's time

It may be noted here that the Indian Meteorology Department has expressed concern that during the recent years, India in general and the North East in particular has received less rain fall in comparison to the average rain fall experienced during the last two decades. So far as the state of Mizoram is concerned, it has been recorded that during January-March, 2009, the state has received 99 p.c. less rain fall than usual rain fall as recorded earlier. We are all aware that global warming, green house effect and climate change continue to be some of the serious threats to our very existence. But it is also a fact that the countries which are responsible for maximum pollution and environmental degradation, show scanty regards for the instruments and action plans like the Kyoto protocol, the Bali declaration and numerous other initiatives advocated worldwide. Some of the supporters of modernisation and development paradigms are of the view that environmental concerns are primarily meant to be the hurdles in the path of progress. There has to be a middle path. We need to develop now. And at the same time we have to address the environmental issues also with a view to creating (or rather leaving behind) a better world order for the future generations.

In this context, the issues and concerns of human security assume special significance.While dealing with the issues of human security particularly in the developing nations, we have to adopt appropriate and environment- friendly technology in such a manner that the basic needs of the people such as food, safe drinking water, basic health care, shelter, primary education and decent livelihood opportunities etc are fulfilled. It is no wonder that most of the political parties in India today face these basic issues in the run up to the elections – both national and state-level. Some of the ruling parties and coalition partners find it a really difficult task to convince the electorate that their developmental agenda is actually environment-friendly.

At the international level, the World Wildlife Fund (WWF), the international organisation, in collaboration with many other national and local level çivil society organisations and nation-states has been organising various programmes and activities to spread awareness about environment and related issues throughout the world. This year their programme "Earth Hour" was observed on March 28, 2009 from 8.30 pm to 9.30 pm (1ST)in as many as 364 cities and towns across the continents. During the Earth Hour, people in these places switched off their electric and electronic gadgets including lights to express their solidarity for the cause of environment and to spread the message of a healthy living in tune with the requirement of environmental balance. In India too many cities joined this endeavour. But we also have a pertinent point to make in this respect. We in India celebrate so many Earth Hours during our scheduled and not so scheduled load shedding hours in different parts of the country throughout the year. We may get some solace from the fact that one of our long standing problems has become a great boon for the cause of environment and has been contributing immensely towards a better future of the entire humanity.

It is to be clearly conceived that when we talk about environmental degradation in India or any part of the world, we should be discussing a number of issues and concerns including that of human generated pollution, industrial waste, urban pollution, eco- system simplification, pollution due to scientific and defence related research in land, air, water, and outer space ; natural resources depletion and such other necessary activities which pose a serious challenge and dilemma before us as to what should be our right course of action. Because in most such cases, the real question is whether to develop or conserve nature. When it comes to fixation of responsibility, at so many factors and forces are involved in the process. Different countries – developed and developing ; individuals – rich and poor; companies – national and multi-national; and so many other individuals and agencies are involved in the process of development which has a direct and negative impact on the health of environment. In the international context, we know that regular forest fire has affected the moisture reservoirs in the African nation of Kenya including the four lakh hectares of

Mau forest reserve, country's largest forest. Incidentally, it is also the source of water for all the twelve major rivers in Kenya including River Nile and Lake Victoria.

An issue which is very closely associated with the question of administration and human security, but at the same time is also concerned with environmental security refers to the socio-economic development of the bulk of the population in most of the developing societies. Unless the nation states are very much pro-active in providing the basic necessities of life to their citizens in terms of food, clothing, shelter, education and decent means of livelihood, there would be social tensions and strife in the society. In the process of development, the states will have to take some concrete measures and action plans which may not be that conducive to the cause of environment. So the question again comes down to the level of whether to go for development or to conserve. And the real issue may be to have sustainable development which refers to an ideal situation under which the present generation would lead a good life in harmony with nature and at the same time would think about the perceptible needs of the future generations to come.

A vast majority of anthropologists and social scientists are of the view that the terms like "human" or 'human beings' stand for neutral concepts which signify rational, autonomous, thinking and seemingly moral actors whom are not at all confined to any area-specific or region-specific constructs like cultural entities or communities. So when we talk about human security as well as environmental security, we are conscious of the fact that people in general and also inside the nation states living anywhere in the world, do think in common and at times act in a unified manner both consciously and otherwise and contribute to the good life and healthy living of the entire humankind along with flora and fauna. The tribal people living in different corners of the world, who worship nature and all things natural, are the pioneers in the field of environmental protection and conservation who should be commended for their so called traditional knowledge and wisdom and who are far more advanced than many of the so called environmentalists and conservationists who create so much hue and cry in support of environmental protection and who are often termed as arm-chair environmentalists.

It is an acclaimed fact that all human beings living in any society of the world, rich or poor, urban or rural, educated or illiterate, developed or developing do require some basic needs and requirements like political liberty, economic equality, social justice, development, fulfillment of the genuine necessities of life, awareness, opportunity to participate in the socio- economic and political life, and empowerment. Any agenda to ensure human security and to provide good life to the people should take into account all these primary issues with a view to embarking on any concrete plan or programme of action. And such plans eventually should consider the environmental aspects as the basic ingredients with critical emphasis on the issues like environmental pollutions and threats, policy initiatives to reverse such activities and the responsibilities of the political executive, the bureaucracy, the civil society, the mass media and the citizens at large in ensuring sustainable development and the best possible practices in terms of environmental protection in any given society and in the best interest of the entire humankind.

While dealing with the issues and concerns of administration in the nation states, we are reminded of the role played by the international community and the institutional arrangements in the field of environmental protection, awareness generation and movement who include, among others, the UN, the UNEP and the UNDP etc along with their partner institutions and organisations. These institutions are multilateral and global in nature and are primarily concerned with the international, global, trans-border impact developmental activities on the environment. They try to harness various resources, agencies, actors and institutions for the promotion and protection of environment and strengthen the multilateral initiatives towards a sustainable future.

When we take note of the role played by the UN agencies in the field of environmental conservation and protection, we generally find that many of these multilateral and international agencies in collaboration with national and regional agencies and institutions look at the environmental discourse from the synergy point of view and normally take a wholesome approach in relation to the needs of life, economy, culture, administration, and development. And it is no wonder to appreciate that these are the very issues which contribute to human security, growth and human development in the world. Unless these issues are tackled in their totality, we would face serious consequences including that of the case of environmental refugees the world over, who may be the direct victims of our developmental process. In this connection, we are reminded of the imperative need of achieving or at least trying to achieve the oft quoted Millennium Development Goals which eventually include the issue of sustainable development.

In India in general and in the North East region in particular, there has been a continuing debate about the nature of economic development. Many of the stakeholders operating either at the national level or at the regional level are of the view that we need to be extra careful while drawing up any developmental plans or programmes. The question of introduction of new railway line in Mizoram and elsewhere in the north eastern region has met with opposition from the ethnic communities as well as from the environmentalists who are of the opinion that all the relevant issues and concerns must be addressed properly before any decision to lay down new railway line is taken in this region which is a vast treasure house in terms of bio- diversity. The recent case of railway expansion in Jammu and Kashmir is a case in point where many experts have opined that with proper planning, environmental concerns could have been addressed better. Again there is another stream of thought which emphasizes on faster economic growth and development of the North East region of India, proponents of this idea are of the view that in the name of environment and future generation, we cannot sacrifice the genuine needs and aspirations of the people of the region who are at present located at the bottom of the development process in India.

We have experienced that the world has come under the influence of a serious economic slowdown or melt down in recent past. Almost all the nations have faced the heat of this grave economic crisis. No country is fully immune from the immediate, medium term and long term impact of the economic slowdown. But there is a silver line among the dark clouds. Experts are of the view that countries like India who have a strong rural base, can benefit from the situation. And we may embark upon a massive plantation activities in the entire country which will serve both the purposes like providing gainful work to the people and creating a healthy environment. In this context, we may refer to the initiative of the Government of India in creating Green India and establishing eight green panels to deal with the aspects of environment vis-a-vis development. The Ministry of Environment and Forest, Government of India, has started a number of initiatives to integrate the processes of planning, implementation, monitoring, and evaluation of different types of developmental activities in the country in close collaboration with their counterparts in the states and also the monitoring agencies operating at the central, state and local levels including the civil societies and pro-active individuals and mass media working for the cause of environmental protection and ecological balance in the country.

It has been reported in the media that the United States, the US Congress has adopted a new enactment to reduce the green house gases to 37 p.c. by AD 2020. This is particularly significant because USA has been one of the largest polluter of the environment among all the nation states. And it is one among the few countries in the world which has been constantly opposing all the global initiatives towards environmental protection by resorting to trivial grounds and at the same time pointing finger at other nations at the slightest pretext. However, there is an encouraging story from within the United States also regarding environmental protection which should be an eye opener for many other countries. The state of California in USA has the enviable track record of maintaining constant per capita consumption of energy during the last thirty-five years.

In India today, a formula is being evolved by the National Climate Action Plan and the National Mission for Energy Efficiency to turn the economic and environmental down-turn into an opportunity. The issue of ensuring institutionalizing energy efficiency standards and energy audits is just a beginning in this field. The Governments of Delhi, Punjab and Haryana have issued strict instructions to their offices to follow conservation norms including a complete ban on the use of air-conditioners in the offices. Green activities within the nation states in such a manner would ensure preparedness among various countries have facilitated negotiations for a new UN sponsored Climate Change Protocol at Copenhagen, Denmark in December 2009 which aimed at negotiating a replacement of the Kyoto Protocol.

We know it for certain that human civilisation and culture would be meaningless without proper environment. Our national and global goals of development may lose their objectives in the absence of a congenial environment. The powers that be operating at different nation states as well as the international organisations will have to take a serious view of the issues like displacement, degradation of habitats, soil erosion and depletion of forest covers etc. while aiming at a better future for the entire human race and not just the greedy life of a few so-called rich states. We need to take a wholesome view of the three interacting factors of politics, planning and progress in the larger interest of the present as well as the future generations. At the same time the nation states have to deal with the pertinent question of a new means of domination i.e., environment which might be used by the already developed nations as a ploy to check the genuine growth requirements of the developing nations. In the final analysis, there has to be a meeting point between environmental security and human security or between the genuine needs of the present and the perceived requirements of the future. The administrative machinery in the states need to be pro-active to address the environmental concerns.

References

Armin Rosencranz. "National Green Tribunal Bill, 2009: Proposal for Improvement", *Economic and Political Weekly,* 44 (48), 2009, November 28, pp. 8-10.

John F. Helliwell, Haifang Huang. "How is your Government? International Evidence linking good government and well-being ", *British Journal of Political science,* 38 (4), October, 2008, pp. 595-619.

Kavita Arora. "Rain forest sustainability in South Asia", *World Affairs,* 12 (1), 2008, Spring, pp. 75-105.

Martin Nie. "The under appreciated role of regulatory enforcement in natural resource conservation", *Policy Science,* 41(2), June, 2008, pp. 139-164.

Paul Wapner, Richard A. Matthew. "The humanity of global environmental ethics", *Journal of Environment and Development,* 18(2), 2009, June, pp. 203-22.

S.L. Goel. *Environmental Health and Value Education,* New Delhi : Deep and Deep, 2008.

Urvashi Dhamija. "Sustainable Solid Waste Management : Issues, Politics and Structures", New Delhi : Academic Foundation, 2008.

R.K. Arora, R.M. Khandelwal (eds.). *Good Governance : Initiatives and Impact,* New Delhi: Paragon International, 2008.

S. Lele, N.K. Dubash, S. Dixit. "A Structure for Environment Governance: A Perspective", *Economic and Political Weekly,* 45 (6), 2010, February 06, pp.13-16.

16

PIL SHOULD VENTILATE PUBLIC INTEREST

V.V. Kanna

In parlance, a person cannot approach a court for redress unless he has **'locus standi'** (the expression used in Britain and India) or **'standing'** (in the US). That is, unless he is the person injured due to act or omission of an individual, a group of persons, a body of corporate or the government. He cannot fight the cause of another who is injured.

The Supreme Court of India and High Courts (aided by Arts. 32 & 226) have taken cognisance of matters brought to their notice by social organisations or individual activists and render justice to the affected persons.

The Supreme Court of India introduced the concept of Public Interest Litigation. The credit of the advent of this Public Interest Litigation era goes to the then Chief Justice Mr. Y.V. Chandrachud, J.J.V.R. Krishna Iyer, P.N. Bhagwati and Justice Chinnappa Reddy. The Public Interest Litigation continued playing vital role in the late 80's and early 90's. The apex court gave all individuals in the country and the newly formed consumer groups or social action groups, an easier access to the law, and introduced in their work a broad public interest perspective.

Public Interest Litigation, popularly known as PIL, can be broadly defined as litigation in the interest of that nebulous entry : the public in general. Prior to the 1980's, only the aggrieved party could knock the doors of justice personally and seek remedy for its grievance and any other person, who was not personally affected, could not approach the judiciary as a proxy for the victim or the aggrieved party.

However, the scenario gradually changed when the post emergency Supreme Court tackled the problem of **'access to justice'** by people through radical changes and alterations made in the requirements of **'locus standi'** and or party aggrieved. The splendid efforts of JJ P.N. Bhagwati and VR K Iyer were instrumental in the juristic revolution of the eighties to convert the apex court of India into a Supreme Court for all Indians. As a result, any citizen of India or any consumer group or social action group can approach the apex court of the country, seeking legal remedies in all cases, where the interests of general public or a section of public are at stake.

In PIL, vigilant citizens of the country can find an inexpensive legal remedy, because there is only a nominal fixed court fee involved in it. Further, through the so called PILs, the litigants can focus attention on and achieve results pertaining to larger public issues, especially in the fields of human rights, consumer welfare and environment. However, the development of Public Interest Litigation has also uncovered its pitfalls and drawbacks. As a result, the apex court itself has been compelled to lay down certain guidelines to govern the management and disposal of the PILs, the abuse of PIL is also increasing along with its extended and multifaceted uses.

The Supreme Court of India is no less aware of the possible abuses of Public Interest Litigation. This is self-evident from various protests within the court in the 1980s, the formulation of self introspective questions in 1983, the elaborate administrative directions regulating letter petitions to the court and a strict examination of whether the petition is simply responding a private cause or publicity. In one case, the court has formally ruled that PIL petitions from a particular lawyer will not be accepted. In the Sheela Barse case, the case proceeded without the involvement of the distinguished journalist who field it. In the Himachal case, anonymous petitions have been rejected. No doubt, the court retains the power to impose heavy costs where the petitions are not bonafide.

With the view to regulating the abuse of Public Interest Litigation, the apex court itself has framed certain guidelines (to governor, the management and disposal of the PILs). The court must be careful to see that the petitioner, who approaches it, is acting bonafide and not for personal gains, private profit or political or other oblique considerations. The court should not allow its process to be abused by politicians or others to delay legitimate administrative action or to gain political objectives, political pressure groups, who could not achieve their aims through the administrative process or political process, may try to use courts (through the means of PILs) to further their closely vested aims and interests.

Public Interest Litigation entails a wide scope of non adversarial inquiry which sometimes carries the court beyond the original reliefs claimed. Courts have by and large, been careful not to enter into roving inquiries unless it is necessitated by the material presented to them. Constitutionally, the right to life and liberty includes the right to ensure governance according to law.

At present, the court can treat a letter as a writ petition and take action upon it. But, it is not every letter which may be treated as a writ petition by the court. The court would be justified in treating the letter as a writ petition only in the following cases: It is only where the letter is addressed by an an aggrieved person or a public spirited individual or a social action group for enforcement of the constitutional or the legal rights of a person, in custody or of a class or group of persons who, by reason of poverty, disability or socially or economically disadvantageous position, find it difficult to approach the court for redress.

In fact, Public Interest Litigation, originally conceived as an instrument of the last recourse, has been trivialised into publicity gestures for pet causes ranging from banning autobiographies, supplying rations to terrorists holed up in Hazratbal and determining the height of Sardar Sarovar Dam to saving the Taj Mahal in India. In election petitions to Mr. Manohar Joshi's 1990 election being a case in point. The courts have been asked to lay down the live political correctness. In the guise of humanitarian concern, NGO's have appealed to the courts to impose restrictive labour practices so as to undermine India's competitive advantage in world trade. A guiltridden intelligentsia has failed to gauge the remarkable conveyance between these apparent displays of humanitarian concern and the back door protectionist agenda of high-cost western economics.

In the landmark case of Raunaq International Ltd. vs. IVR Constructions Ltd., Justice Sujatha V Manohar rightly enunciated that "when a stay-order is obtained at the instance of a body litigating in public interest, any interim order which stop the project from proceeding further must provide for the reimbursement of costs to the public, in case ultimately the litigation started by such an individual or body fails". In other words, the public must be compensated both for the delay in the implementation of the project and the cost escalation resulting from such delay.

Now-a-days Public Interest Litigants all over the country have not taken very kindly to such court decisions. They do fear that this will sound the death knell of the 'people friendly' concept of PIL. However, bonafide litigants of India have nothing to fear. In any way, PIL now does require a complete rethink and restructuring. Over-use and abuse of the PILs can only make them stale and ineffective. Since it is an extraordinary remedy available at a cheaper cost to all the citizens of the country, it ought not to be used by all litigants as a substitute for ordinary ones or as a means to file frivolous complaints.

It may be concluded that public interest petition maintainable even where no public interest is involved or suffered. PIL has been an invaluable innovative judicial remedy. Courts must realise that judicial tyranny is worse than executive or legislative tyranny. But the remedy lies not in bringing in legislation to curb Public Interest Litigation but in leaving it to the good sense of the courts to exercise their jurisdiction only in proper cases. One should admit that PIL has translated the rhetoric of fundamental rights into living reality for at least some segments or our exploited and downtrodden humanity.

References

1. *Deccan Chronicle Newspaper*, May 6th, 1995. (SC to Sssue guidelines on Public Interest Litigation)
2. *Indian Express Newspaper*, March 1st, 1996 (Short cuts to fame, by Swapan Das Gupta)
3. Upendra Baxi, Indian Supreme Court and Politics, 1980.
4. Justice D.A. Desai, 'Constitutional Values and Judicial Activism', 1982.
5. *The Hindu Newspaper*, 28th Feb., 1997.
6. Tarkunde, V.M. (2000), "Democracy and Human Rights", in S. Meharta J. Begum (ed), Human Rights in India, New Delhi, APH Publishing House.

17

THE PARADIGM OF PUBLIC - PRIVATE PARTNERSHIP IN URBAN LOCAL GOVERNANCE IN ANDHRA PRADESH

Ch. Bala Ramulu and *P. Narasimha Rao*

Introduction

The governance, in general terms, may be referred to the action or manner of governing, administering, conducting affairs, etc. of an organisation. In the context of public organisations, the governance may be referred to as setting of rules, the application of rules and the enforcement of rules for the well being of the society. The economic liberalisation and privatisation, initiated during 1980's, in United Kingdom and other countries, have brought about a transformation in economic systems, governance and practices world over. The most important change in the governance model i.e. Public - Private Partnership (PPP) which is fast catching up among most of the developing countries, including India. The new economic reforms introduced in India in 1991 compelled the Central, State and Local Governments to adopt new administrative models/methods to provide public infrastructural facilities and services to the people.

PPP is considered as an important model of governance specifically targeted towards financing, designing, implementing and operating infrastructural facilities and services that were traditionally provided by the public sector. This collaborative arrangement is built around the expertise and capability of partners. Under this arrangement, the Private sector – a private company or a non-governmental organisation (NGO) or a foreign state – owned enterprise or a consortium – participation is expected to bring in technical and managerial expertise, improve operational efficiency, enfus financial resources and introduce competitiveness.

Under PPP approach, the skills, expertise and experience of both public and private sectors get combined to deliver higher standard of service to the customers. The government contributes assurance in terms of appropriate policy, incentives, stable governance, citizen's support, finance and confidence to the private sector to invest on a massive scale and also meet the environmental and political risks. This approach also assures that private sector brings along operational efficiencies, innovative technologies, managerial effectiveness, access to additional finances, and bears construction, commercial and operational risk of the project. Thus, PPP is a contract between public and private sector to deliver higher standards of services/goods to the people.

Review of Literature

The studies on PPP strategies reveal that the privatisation of public services resulted in cost and price reduction; improved quality and delivery of services; raising of resources for governments; reduction in the size of State/Local Governments and economy of scale (Ghuman, B.S. and Mahata, A, 2010).

However, certain studies also documented the issues/ problems involved in the PPP strategies. They highlighted that the benefits of PPP model are temporary phenomena. In the long run privatisation of public services leads to hike in costs and prices; poor quality of services; inefficiency; inequity; unemployment; and corruption. The major reasons for this are: nexus between officials and contractors; faulty contract design; lack of clarity on the control and performance of the contractors; interference of political parties in the granting of contracts, etc., collectively accounted for unsatisfactory outcomes of privatisation of public services.

History of PPP in India

India has few notable PPPs as early as in the 19th century. The Great Indian Peninsular Railway Company operating between Bombay (now Mumbai) and Thana (now Thane) (1953), the Bombay Tramway Company running tramway Services in Bombay (1874), and the power generation and distribution companies in Bombay and Calcutta (now Kolkata) in the early 20th century are some of the earliest examples of PPP in India. Since the opening of economy in 1991, there have been several cautious and tentative attempts at PPP in India. However, most PPPs have been restricted to a few sectors like roads and water supply. Despite becoming the second fastest growing and the fourth largest economy of the world, India continues to face large gaps in the demand and supply of essential social and economic infrastructure and services. Rapidly growing economy, increased industrial activity, burgeoning population pressure, and all-round economic and social development have led to greater demand for better quality and coverage of water and sanitation services, sewerage and drainage systems, solid-waste management, roads and seaports, and power supply. Increased demand has put the existing infrastructure under tremendous pressure and has far outstripped its supply.

Recent Trends

The Government of India and State Governments have articulated its commitment to promote PPPs in almost all the key infrastructure sectors of transport, power, urban infrastructure, and tourism, including railways. Behind the increasing thrust of the government is the growing realisation that lack of social development in India: and to rapidly scale up good-quality infrastructure, a very large investment is required; which cannot be financed by the government's limited budgetary resources and constrained borrowing capacity. These shortcomings are best addressed by bringing in private capital, expertise, entrepreneurial spirit, and techno managerial efficiencies. The infrastructure shortages are proving to be the leading binding constraints in sustaining, deepening and expanding India's economic growth and competitiveness. This has also been emphasised in the mid-term appraisal of the Tenth Five Year Plan. It is widely believed that lack of good quality infrastructure is costing India one to two per cent growth in gross domestic product (GDP) every year.

Lack of infrastructure is preventing the sectoral, regional, and socio-economic broadening of the economy and its benefits, and is affecting inclusive growth in India. The benefits of accelerated growth of the last decade failed to reach to the large sections of the population which are labour dependent, low skilled, rural based, and working in agriculture and manufacturing sectors. Infrastructure shortages have slowed the growth of manufacturing industries and agriculture, which are the labour-absorbing markets for the low skilled. Poverty levels remain significant, with about one-fourth of the population living in poverty. Infrastructure is now seen as the necessary conditions for growth and poverty alleviation. Rural roads, rural electrification and irrigation networks, power grids, and national highways have the potential to link poor rural producers to their power sources and markets in towns, cities and ports. Greater investments in infrastructure are the answers arrived for these problems.

However, successfully working PPP models are a more recent phenomenon. The Tirupur project in Tamil Nadu is a shining example. It is a BOOT project, the first privately financed water and sewerage project in India. The Project took more than ten years from concept to financial closure. The US$ 100 million Delhi-NOIDA Bridge Project, implemented on a facilitating PPP / BOOT framework on the basis of a 30 years concession, is India's first major PPP initiative. The NOIDA toll bridge, Tirupur water supply and sanitation projects are yet to demonstrate their commercial viability to the public. Absence of regulatory authorities and the desired legal framework in the water supply and sanitation sector are some of the hurdles in the way of PPP.

The Central, State and Local governments have been undertaking projects in different public sectors/services like health, education, irrigation, power, roads, airports, communication, urban civic amenities etc under PPP. The governments are working on a number of initiatives to assist and encourage capacity building at the state and central levels. It is identifying the capacity building needs of state governments, providing assistance for the creation of state-level PPP cells as nodal agency, streamlining their approval process, developing PPP toolkits, model concession agreements (MCAs), project manuals, bidding documents, and preparation manuals. It is also building a central database and website on PPPs to disseminate updated information to the states and the private sector. Arrangements are being finalised under which state governments would be able to avail of consultancy support for developing PPP projects.

The experience with the PPP in public sector is nearly two decades and it is the time to examine the strengths and weakness of this approach to development and judge whether it holds good in future. This is more important in the context of the recent economic crisis and doubts in the capacity of corporate governance in undertaking projects under PPP.

The Local Governance and PPP

The 73rd and 74th CA Acts envisage that the local governments – rural and urban have to provide basic amenities to the people. The broad objectives of decentralised rural governance are to: (i) plan and execute schemes to meet local needs; (ii) mobilise people and channelise their energies towards socio-economic reconstruction and to involve them in all activities of the communities through the new institutions; (iii) reduce the work of the higher levels of government and making the people responsible to decide their destiny; (iv) ensure welfare, equality, equity and social well-being; (v) ensure honesty among the bureaucracy and transparency in the administration; (vi) eradication of corruption; (vii) make administration more efficient and citizen focused; (viii) ensure that fruits of development reach deep down the society; (ix) reduce economic, social and regional disparities; (x) ensure transparency and quick decision-making; (xi) develop network among rural organisations for the development of the country or area; (xii) emphasise democratic governance for economic and human development; and (xiii) reorient, reinvent and restructure public institutions. The World Bank's notion of: "Governance is the institutional capacity of public organisations to provide the public and other goods demanded by country's citizens or their representatives in an effective, transparent, impartial, and accountable manner, subject to resource constraints." The rural local governments are also adopting PPP model to realise its objectives.

The unprecedented growth of urbanisation has put service strain on the government's capacity, particularly urban local government to provide services to the rapidly increasing urban population. The urban governments are fast approaching for PPP to provide basic facilities to the people. The governance of PPP is expected to: prepare regulatory policy and detailed planning; guide and supervise the affairs of the projects; ensure price certainty and cost effectiveness; deliverence of qualitative goods and services; transparency impartial and accountability; ensure access, equity and quality of services to all people and regions; protect the interest of stakeholders; execute the schemes to meet local needs; enhance the capacity of organisation and make more efficient and citizen-focused; etc.

PPP in Urban Local Governments

In India, the process of Urbanisation has been gaining

momentum. The urban population grew at the rate of 2.73 per cent per annnum between the period of 1991 and 2001. According to 2001 census, urban population constituted 27.8 per cent of the population. Though less than one-third people of India reside in urban areas, but in terms of absolute number, the urban population comes around 285.4 million. This number poses challenges to the urban local bodies to provide public service to the people.

The public services provided by urban local bodies (ULB) however, could not keep pace with the growing urban population. Majority of the ULBs across the country have been facing severe financial hardships and hence fail to provide adequate and quality public services including urban infrastructure to their citizens. Private capital has been invited by a number of ULBs for providing civic services to the people. The process of privatisation of public services in urban areas got a fillip after the introduction of economic liberalisation policy of 1991 (Ghuman, B.S. and others, 2010).

Jawaharlal Nehru National Urban Renewal Mission:

The Jawaharlal Nehru National Urban Renewal Mission (JNNURM) was launched on 3rd December 2005 with an investment of Rs. 50,000 crores in the mission period of seven years beginning 2005-06. The mission is the single largest initiative of the Government of India for planned urban development that integrates the two pressing needs of urban India: massive investments required for infrastructure development reforms that are required to sustain investments. The primary object of the mission is to create economically productive, efficient, equitable and responsive cities. To achieve this objective, it focuses on integrated development of infrastructure services; securing linkages between asset creation and maintenance for long-run project sustainability; accelerating the flow of investment into urban infrastructure services; planned urban development; renewal of inter-city areas and universalisation of urban services to ensure balanced urban development (Debolina Kundu and Dibyendu Samnata, 2011).

It aims to encourage reforms and fast-track infrastructure development with a focus on efficiency in urban infrastructure and services delivery mechanism, community participation and accountability of ULBs to the people. The JNNURM has two sub-missions for the mission cities viz (1) Urban Infrastructure and Governance (UIG) (2) Basic Services to the Urban Poor (BSUP). Under these programmes, the city governance is expected to create conditions through reform measures and infrastructural investment in 65 select cities for attracting domestic and foreign investment. In the case of non-mission towns and cities, the JNNURM is expected to provide assistance under two major components, viz., the (i) UIG of the Urban Infrastructure Development Schemes for small and medium Towns (UIDSSMT) and (ii) The Integrated Housing and Slum Development Programme (IHSDP). The mission activities are operationalised by PPP mode.

The studies on the performance of JNNURM reveal that a little over half of the Urban Population (58%) has been covered under the mission. However, the coverage varies from one State to other. The Coverage is more in the developed states and metropolitan cities, compared to backward States and Cities. The budget allocation also indicates that the developed States and big Cities are availing more budgets under JNNURM.

An Analysis of the information regarding the projects and schemes launched under the UIG component in different cities reveal that most of these have been designed to increase the total capacity of the basic urban services – Water supply, Sanitation and Sewerage– at the city level. There is no explicit provision to improve the access of the poor to these services. Given the emphasis on reform, financial efficiency and cost recovery for each of the facilities (collecting user charges) and promotion of public-private partnership, it is understandable that those who have affordability will corner much of the benefits from this augmented system. This would further increase the spatial disparity within cities (Kundu.D and others, 2011).

The studies also point out that the annual per capita spending by the central government on different schemes meant for mission and non-mission cities/towns is more in favour of the creation of urban infrastructure and governance (UIG) than providing Basic Services to the Urban Poor (BSUP). The annual per capita fund released to the UIG is Rs.153, while it is Rs.66 to the BSUP. Similarly, the annual per capita funds released under UIG UIDSSMT is Rs.78, while it is Rs.40 under IHSDP. The annual per capita funds released under all the urban development schemes works to be Rs.165, while it is Rs.52 for pro-poor component activities (Kundu.D and others, 2011).

Another problem in the JNNURM is that there is a wide gap between the budget allocation and release of funds. The studies high light that less than half of the total allocations (45.5%) have been released under JNNURM to the cities/ towns for infrastructure development and housing the poor.

PPP in Urban Governance in Andhra Pradesh

In Andhra Pradesh there are 110 urban local bodies of which 16 are municipal corporations. The Government is also planning to upgrade some of municipalities and major panchayats as municipal corporations and municipalities, respectively. The Government intention is to give priority to attract funds from private institutions and other agencies to develop infrastructure in the urban areas and also provide civic amenities to the citizens.

Delivery of Public Services in AP

The urban local bodies in AP, during more than one and a half decades, are adopting the PPP model of governance to meet the demands of the people. It has initiated reforms involving private sector participation in the provision of municipal services, particularly in the cities like Hyderabad, Visakhapatanam, and Tirupathi. Around 31 percent of civic services provided by 108 in the state have been contracted out. This process further accentuate with the launching of JNNURM in big cities mentioned above. The public services which are privatised/contracted out include: lifting and transforming of garbage, night sanitation, desilting of drains, maintenance of street lighting, maintenance of parks and annual exhibition, finalisation of accounts collection of advertisement tax, cleaning of roads, streets, meter reading, data entry and processing, construction and maintenance of bus shelters, ward security, market development, mid-day meals programme, development of tourism, development house-sites/colonies, construction of buildings and shopping complex and its maintenance, laying of roads water supply - portable drinking water supply in slum areas, up gradation of infrastructure and its operation and maintenance and construction of culverts and bridges, flyovers, construction of community halls and maintenance of traffic signals, burial grounds, public toilets, equipments, staff buildings, and quarters, regularisation of natural streams, play grounds and stadiums, subways and causeways, foot over bridges, construction of dhobi ghats, etc. operation and maintainers, etc. Earlier all these services were provided by urban local bodies and authorities.

Performance of PPP Mode of governance in Urban Areas in AP

The urban local bodies/authorities' reports reveal that many of the public services are privatised and huge budget is allocated for construction and maintenance of the assets/ equipments/services. The basic infrastructural facilities and services are improved in the cities. The foreign direct investment in basic sectors/service sector, private capital and above all the migration of rural people to the cities in search of livelihood and the availability of large and qualitative services posing major challenges to the urban local bodies/ authorities. Further, this trend also is causing a nightmare to the people to live in the city.

The experience with PPP strategy in the big cities is not all encouraging. The major hurdles are: unrealistic design of the projects; manipulation in granting contracts to execute the projects, overestimation of the budget of the projects leading to wastage of money and resources, delay in release of budget by the municipal authorities to the private executors, legal hurdles in executing the projects; appointment of employees on contract basis, who have low level of commitment; underpayment to the workers /employees by the contractors; manipulation of service records and payment to the outsourced employees; poor quality of services/ facilities to the slum dwellers or low-lying areas, concentration of services/facilities in the areas which are relatively better endowed areas; monopoly of certain individuals in getting contracts for execution of the works/services etc. All these factors and several other factors are collectively defeating the major initiative of PPP mode of governance, which is aimed at economically productive, efficient, equitable and responsive to the citizens.

Conclusion

The above analysis reveals that the urban local bodies/ authorities are withdrawing its social and economic responsibilities and assigning them to the private sector. This is partly due to the resource constraints and partly ever increasing urban population. The public private partnership mode of governance has become an inevitable process in providing services to the citizens, mostly in big cities. The urban renewal / reforms / programmes like JNNURM is also encouraging this PPP mode in the creation of infrastructure and delivery of services to the people. The new economic partner foreign direct investment and private sector investment in industry/service sector have further accentuated the process of PPP mode of governance to meet the challenges in the delivery of services to the people. This is more so in the metropolitan cities like Hyderabad.

The analysis also unfolds that the urban renewal reforms (JNNURM) instead of bringing inclusive growth in the urban areas, have contributed for widening disparities between the cities and within the city/ies, as the allocation of funds and utilisation of funds is more to the big cities of developed states, compared to the towns/municipalities both in the developed and backward states. The experience of PPP mode of governance in Andhra Pradesh is no different to that of other areas. The performance of this model is not encouraging. Though this strategy has contributed for creation of additional infrastructure like flyovers, international airport, outer ring roads, development of residential colonies, and providing basic services to the slum dwellers, etc.; basic issues like control of corruption, monopoly of contractors; enabling the poor access to the basic services; providing timely and quality of services to the people remain unresolved even to date. Thus the privatisation of public services is not a panacea for all the ills of urban local authorities or alternative to providing services to the people through the urban local bodies. It is time for the central and state governments and urban local bodies to re-look into the problems/issues that crop up in the PPP strategy in providing services to the people and take necessary initiatives to make the urban growth process more inclusive.

References

1. Debolina Kundu and Dibyendu Samnata, (2011). Redefining the inclusive urban agenda in India, *Economic and Political Weekly,* No. 5 Vol. 46. pp. 55 to 63.
2. Ghuman, B.S. and others, (2010). Privatisation of Public Services by Urban Local Governments in India–A case study of Municipal Council of Phankula, *Nagarlok*, Vol. XLII, January-March, 2010, pp. 50 to 68.

18

EMPOWERMENT OF WOMEN THROUGH SHGS MOVEMENT

T. Yadagiri Rao

Human resource development plays a critical role in the socio-economic development of a country. It is an investment towards improving the quality of human life. Although development brings economic gains to society in general, specific measures become necessary to ensure that they reach the disadvantaged and the weaker sections of the population such as women, children, disabled, elderly and the destitute. The welfare and development of these weaker sections of the society largely depend upon suitable policy directions executed through appropriate programmes and strategies.

Women and children, who represent more than two-third (67.7%) of the India's total population constitute the important target groups in the context of the present day. Most of the scholars have attracted towards women development programmes in India. The governments are making the legislation on the basis of public opinion. Public policy is nothing but the promises made by the political parties at the time of elections. Women and child development activities are the challenging tasks for the modern government, particularly for Indian government. Education of the women and children has been recognised as a leading task for their growth and empowerment.

Empowerment has multiple dimensions, which are inter related viz. social, economic, political and capability development. The empowerment process encompasses several mutually reinforcing components supported by economic independence, which implies access to land control over production resources. A second component of employment is knowledge and awareness. The third one is self image and self esteem. The ultimate compound is self autonomy. The empowering women put the spot light on their health, education and employment. These are all an essential components for independent and sustainable growth and development of the women.

The principles of gender equality and equity and protection of women's rights have been the prime concerns in Indian thinking right from the days of independence. Accordingly, the country's concern in safeguarding the rights and privileges of women found its best expression in the Constitution of India. While Article 14 confers equal rights and opportunities on men and women in the political economic and social spheres, Article 15 prohibits discrimination against any citizen on the grounds of sex, religion, race, caste, etc. and Article 15(3) empowers the state to make affirmative discrimination in favour of women. Similarly, Article 16 provides for equality of opportunities in the matter of public appointments for all citizens. Article 39 mentions that the state shall direct its policy towards providing men and women equally the right to means of livelihood and equal pay for equal work and maternity relief. Article 51(a)(c) imposes a fundamental duty on every citizen to renounce the practices derogatory to the dignity of women.

Women development programmes were started from the starting of first five year plan (1951) onwards. In the initial years of planning era, the welfare-oriented strategy was adopted for women's development in India. The growth-oriented model of development, it was assumed, will automatically distribute equitably the fruits of development to all sections of the society including women.

During the 1980s, the Government of India adopted a multi- disciplinary approach with a special thrust on three core sectors of health, education and employment. Accordingly, priority was given to implementation of programmes for women under different sectors of agriculture and its allied activities of dairying, poultry, animal husbandry, handlooms, handicrafts, small scale industries etc. Recognising the role and contribution of women in development, the early nineties made a beginning in concentrating on training-cum-employment cum-income generation programmes with the ultimate objective of making them economically independent and self reliant.

The present participatory planning process recognises women as an active agent of socio-economic change, hence it adopted integrated approach for the empowerment of women. The present strategy perceives that the women are not only active participants but also real partners in the process of development rather than treating them as passive beneficiaries, by allowing them to participate freely in productive and entrepreneurial capabilities in the fullest possible manner.

Women Welfare Programmes in Five Year Plans

The government of India under the different five years plans has taken up various welfare and development schemes for the welfare of women. The first five year plan (1951-56) envisaged welfare measures for the women for this purpose. The Central Social Welfare Board (CSWB) was established in 1953 to promote and assist voluntary organisations in the field of women welfare, child welfare and welfare of the handicapped. The second Five Year Plan (1956-61) given priority for women issues, particularly the women workers. Under the community development programme, Mahila Mandals were promoted and supported. Third and fourth plans accorded a high priority to education to women, measures to improve maternal and child health services.

The fifth five year plan supported economic development. The main approach in this plan was generally to view women as the beneficiaries of social services rather than as the contributors to development. During the sixth five year plan, a multi sectoral approach was adopted for women's development and for the first time a coordinated picture was presented in the plan.

A separate Department of Women's welfare was carved out at the Centre in 1985 since the then existing Ministry of Social and Women's Welfare to give a separate identity and to provide a nodal point on matters relating to women's development. Legislative measures were taken to provide protection to women against discrimination, exploitation, atrocities and violence. Various labour legislations were amended to safeguard the interests of women and provide for their welfare.

FRom the seventh five year plan continued the women developmental programme. The National Perspective Plan for Women (1988-2000) provided directions for all-round development of women. The National Commission on self-employed women and women in informal sector submitted a comprehensive report titled "Shramshakti", analysing the problems affecting a large number of women in the informal sector and steps needed to give them a better deal.

In the seventh plan towards improving women's status, was the identification of a number of beneficiary-oriented programmes under various sectors' development. These programmes were regularly monitored by the concerned departments and coordinated at the center by the Department of Women and Child Development.

The landmark achievement of both the 73rd and 74th Constitutional Amendment in 1993 brought forth a definite impact on the participation of women in the grass-root democracy through Panchayati Raj Institutions (PRls) and Local Bodies. In the election of PRls held during 1993-95, women have achieved participation even beyond the mandatory requirement of 1/3rd of total seats in the states like West Bengal (35.1%) Kerala (36.4%) and Karanataka (43.4%). In fact these amendments are expected to achieve effective participation of women in grass-root democratic Institutions and its processes, both as individuals and as representatives of interest groups.

Human development being the major thrust in the Eighth Five Year Plan (1992-97), the plan sought to ensure that the number of benefits from other development sectors did not bypass women and the same was monitored with a special vigil in the three core sectors of health, education, and employment. To this effect, the special mechanism of monitoring the 27 Beneficiary Oriented Programmes for women was continued in the eighth five year plan. It envisaged that women must be enabled to function as equal partners and participants in the country's developmental process. This approach of the eighth plan marks a shift from development to empowerment of women. Improvement in the health status of women received high priority during the eighth plan.

Empowerment of Women's being one of the nine primary objectives of the ninth plan, efforts are made to create an enabling environment where women can freely exercise their rights both within and outside home, as equal partners along with men. This will be realised through early finalisation and adoption of the 'National Policy for Empowerment of Women' which laid down definite goals, targets and policy prescription along with a well-defined Gender Development Index to monitor the import of its implementation in raising the status of women.

Organising Self-Help Groups (SHGs)

While organizing women into self-help groups, marks the beginning of a major process of empowering women. The institutions thus developed would provide a permanent forum for articulating the women's needs and contributing their perspectives to developments. Recognising the fact that women have been socialised only to take a back seat in public life, alternative action through deliberate strategies will be initiated to provide equal access to and control over factors contributing to such empowerment, vocational skills, employment and income generating opportunities, land and other forms of property including through inheritance, common property, resources, credit, technology and market etc.

To this effect, the newly elected women members and the women chairpersons of panchayats and the local bodies will be sensitised through the recently launched special training package to take the lead in ensuring that adequate funds/ benefits flow towards the empowerment of women and girl child.

The Ninth plan recognised the need for a conducive Credit Policy to increase the access for women to credit through appropriate institutional mechanisms like Rashtriya Mahila Kosh (RMK), National Agricultural Bank for Rural Development (NABARD), Council for Advancements of Peoples Action and Rural Technology (CAPART), Women cooperatives SHGs and the other financial institutions. In this context, expansion of the activities of Rashtriya Mahila Kosh (RMK) need special attention. Efforts will also be made to learn lessons from the success stories of various voluntary organisation who have already established their all credentials in the field of credit and encourage them to expand their activities, both within and outside their status.

The Approach to the Tenth Five Year Plan elucidates the fact that women are the most vulnerable group within every category. Thus there is an urgent need to review the outcomes and impacts of on-going programmes of "social safety nets" for women, and redesign them as necessary to ensure that they advance gender equality goals.

In order to improve the well-being of women and children in the society, the Government has made a significant shift in the approach from "Welfare during Fifties" to "Development during Seventies" and to "Empowerment during the Nineties". During the nineties major thrust in respect of women was to make them economically independent and self-reliant, while in respect of children efforts were made to ensure their 'survival', 'protection' and 'development' with special focus on the girl child and adolescent girl.

The vision of the Eleventh Five Year Plan is to end the multifaceted exclusions and discriminations faced by women and children; to ensure that every woman and child in the country are able to develop their full potential and share the benefits of economic growth and prosperity. Success will depend on our ability to adopt a participatory approach that empowers women and children and makes them partners in their own development. The roadmap for this has already been laid in the National Policy on Women 2001 and the National Plan of Action for Children 2005.

The ultimate objective of all these efforts is to make women economically independent and self reliant. Some of the important initiatives thus undertaken in this direction include launching of programmes viz. work and wage, 'learn while you earn', credit for Entrepreneurial/self-employment ventures, Employment Guaranty schemes etc. both in rural and urban areas. While programmes like IMY (Indira Mahila Yojana), DWCRA (Development of women and children in rural areas), STEP (Support for training and Employment) TEPC (Training cum employment cum production centre) popularly known as NORAD are some of the important women specific employment-cum training programmes.

There exists a few more programmes like IRDP (Integrated Rural Development Programme), TRYSEM (training of rural youth for self employment programmes), JRY (Jawahar Rojgar Yojana), NRY (Nehru Rojgar Yojana), PMRY (Prime Minister's Rojgar Yojana) which extend 30 to 40% reservation of benefits for women.

Empowerment through SHGs

The Government of India evolved several policies for the

women's advancement in the society, one such policy is DWCRA, later on changed its nomenclature as SHGs through several safeguards and enactments are provided to women since the government of India decided to eliminate the gender bias and the same time providing economic security by allowing them to participate in the economic activity. The concept of SHGs is considered as a multifaceted strategy or approach to improve the status and standard of living of the rural women.

The following are the objectives of the SHGs:

1. Educating themselves
2. In supporting each other
3. In solving day-to-day problems
4. In strengthening their own particular socio-economic status
5. Increase in Self-confidence and self-esteem

This programme is intended to cover the rural poor. The purpose of this programme is not only to improve the economic status of the rural women providing credit facilities and providing self employment opportunities. The recommendations of the Planning Commission Expert Committee suggested for the convergence of different self employment programmes into a single programme i.e. Swarna Jayanthi Gram Swarojgar, later on it became as groups.

There are about 4.65 lakhs women SHGs in Andhra Pradesh covering nearly 61.70 lakhs poor women. Andhra Pradesh alone has about half of SHGs organised in the Country. The SHGs are also popularly called DWCRA Groups, and this name became popular after the DWCRA programme (Development of Women and Children in Rural Areas) through which women's groups were assisted initially. The SHGs are not only resorting to thrift but also are taking small loans out of the corpus available with the group. The group corpus consists of savings, government assistance and also bank loan. Members use the loan out of group corpus for their personal needs initially. In the long run such loans are utilised for income generation activities. So far an amount of Rs.1556.90 crores is mobilised as corpus by these groups.

Micro credit to SHGs

Micro credit summit conducted in 1997 in Washington resolved to reach 100 million poor women by 2005 all over the world. In Andhra Pradesh alone, 61.70 lakh women were covered under micro credit with a saving of a rupee per day and the financial institutions extending loans upto 4 times to the amount of group savings. From 1997 to January 2003, Banks extended a loan of Rs.1345 crores to SHG and the recovery of loans is more than 95%. Recently commercial banks have reduced interest rate on the loans extended to SHGs from 12% to 9%.

Expansion of SHGs at grass root level

All the villages in A.P. have at least one SHG and 75% of the villages have 15-20 groups in each. The Government felt the necessity of building institutions for SHG at the village and mandal level ('Mandal' is an administrative unit equivalent 1/3 size of a block). Village organisations and mandal federations are formed and the latter are registered under the mutually aided co-operative societies Act 1995. Such federations take up functions like pensions to old people, insurance services to members, procurement of raw materials and marketing of finished products, accessing community infrastructure facilities, providing market information and other services to the members.

Economic Empowerment of SHGs

Sixty per cent of the women take up economic activities related to agriculture and allied activities. Land lease for growing agricultural crop is a common practice in 9 Telangana districts. Vegetable and Flower cultivation, food crops and pulses, oil seeds cultivation are taken up on leased lands. Similarly, rearing of calves, ram lamb, chicks, piggery and duckery, dairy, value addition to milk and milk products are preferred by women agricultural labourers. Illiterate and unskilled women engage in small business activities. Nearly 20% of the SHG members are artisans and engaged in making handicrafts and handloom products.

Public private partnership method is adopted in promoting economic opportunities to SHG members by appointing them as dealers for the sale of prodcts manufactured by companies like Hindustan Levers Limited, TVS, TTK-Prestige, Colgate-Palmolive, Philips etc. Companies in return train SHGs in finance management, enterprise development, packaging, branding and pricing of products. This partnership is a win win model.

Andhra Pradesh is now engaged in intense pursuit of development prgrammes utilising information technology (IT) and to strategies as to how the benefits of IT could be taken to rural areas. SHGs are encouraged to get PCs and software for accessing information and developing their business. Their products are photographed, scanned and displayed on websites. These are put on the portals of e-commerce companies. Handicrafts, herbal medicines and cosmetics, hand woven and embroidered curtains, toys, paintings etc., are thus finding national and international markets. This would not have been possible, but for the internet. The members are enabled to take a mobile telephone and use it not only for the sales but as a public telephone.

Impact of SHG Movement

Various organisations like NGOs, universities, National Bank for Agricultural & Rural Development (NABARD) and ORG-Marg evaluated SHGs. Some of the salient features found are:

- 98% of the members make savings regularly as per the norms prescribed by the groups.
- All the groups meet at least once in a month to discuss various social issues related to their day to day life.
- 98% of eligible members adopt small family norms.

- 100% children of SHG members are able to access immunisation services against six diseases.
- 30% of the members have access to safe cooking fuels (LPG) under the Government promoted scheme popularly known as "DEEPAM".
- 80% of the total SHGs have accessed financial assistance from banks and repayment is 98%.
- 10,000 SHG members were elected to the local bodies (3 tier Panchayat Raj Institutions) in 1997 November elections.
- Members are engaged in 450 varieties of income generating activities.

Voluntary participation in community activities like laying roads, planting trees conserving environment, construction of water harvesting structures, donations to the victims of natural calamities helping to reduce crime against girls and women, campaign against eradication of social evils like dowry, child marriages, untouchability, AIDS, rescue and rehabilitation of orphaned children, counseling adolescent girls, support to widows and destitutes are a few to mention. SHG members learning from the past experiences are walking through the present and marching ahead for a bright future.

Conclusion

The SHG programmes members possess rural base and bias who came to equip with given financial potency to invest on their income generation activities in order to avoid the exploitation of the rural money lenders. The government initiated women programmes DWCRA and Self Help Group programmes were successful in achieving the declared objectives, mainly eradication of poverty and unemployment of the rural women and empowering the weaker section women in the rural areas. The Self Help Groups were adopted as a viable alternative to individual approach focused in earlier programmes. The SHG programme enhanced the general knowledge and awareness and improved the bargaining capacity of the rural women. Their economic status has been enormously increased and it indicates that rural women are fully equipped with empowerment in all respects. It is proved that if rural women are socially, economically and politically developed they try to eradicate anti-development customs and help for implementation of development programmes by the government. After joining and working with SHG, there is enormous attitudinal change of approach in a very positive looking towards the girl child and they opposed the feticide and sex determination tests and they try to eradicate the caste system and help to establish the social justice. It can be concluded that after becoming the members of the self-help groups, the women acquired self confidence and maintaining self image and self esteem for excellence. Hence, SHG programmes immensely improved the status and prestige of rural women. This impact can be seen in the form of empowerment of rural women.

References

1. Gopal Singh, *et al.* : "Economic Empowerment of Rural Women in India", RBSA Publication, Jaipur, 2003.
2. Kumaran, K.P. : "Case Studies on Self-Help Groups", www.nird.gov.in, Research Highlights, 1997.
3. Singh, A.K. *Empowerment of Women in India*, Mank Publications, 2000.
4. Neera Burra, Joy Deshmukh-Ranadive and Ranjani K. Murthy. 'Micro-Credit, Poverty and Empowerment: Linking the triad'. Sage Publications, 2005.
5. K.G. Karmakar, 'Rural Credit and Self-Help Groups: Micro-finance needs and concepts in India', Sage Publications, 1999.
6. 'SHGs help to promote women entrepreneurship'. *The Hindu*, Jan 24, 2005.

7. 'SHG movement takes a leap forward', *The Hindu*, September 30, 2005.

8. Meenakshi Anand Chaudhary. "Empowerment Strategies for Rural Women in India", *Kurukshethra*, March 1996.

9. Rekha, R. Gaonkar. "Working and Impact of Self-Help Groups in Goa". *Indian Journal of Agricultural Economics*, July-September, 2001.

19

GUJJARS MOVEMENT IN RAJASTHAN–A STUDY

Devath Suresh

Gujjars are mainly concentrated in the Indo-Gangetic plains, the Himalayan region, and eastern parts of Afghanistan. A majority of *Gujjars* follow Hinduism and Islam. In India, *Gujjar* populations are found mainly in Gujarat, Delhi, Jammu and Kashmir, Himachal Pradesh, Punjab, western Uttar Pradesh, Uttarakhand, Haryana, northern Madhya Pradesh, Rajasthan and Maharashtra. The semi- nomadic *Gujjar* groups are found in the states of Jammu and Kashmir, Himachal Pradesh, and north-western Uttar Pradesh. The name for the state of Gujarat has derived from *"Gurjar". Gujari (or Gojri)*, classified under Rajasthani, has traditionally been the primary language of the *Gujjars*. But, *Gujjars* living in different areas speak several other languages including Hindi, Marathi, Urdu, Punjabi, *Pothohari, Pahari* languages (such as *Dogri* and *Kangri*), Pashto language, *Dardic* languages (such as *Kashmiri* and *Khowar*), and *Balti*. *Gujjars* in North India are now considered as a vote bank by some political parties. The *Gujjars* were classified as a Scheduled Tribe in Himachal Pradesh and Jammu & Kashmir, and as Other Backward Class in Rajasthan, Haryana, Madhya Pradesh and Uttar Pradesh.[1]

Most of the people in India, especially in the south and the east, had no knowledge that there is a community called

Gujjars (or *Gurjjars*). Till December, 21st to 27th December 2010, probably no one who follows the media would be unaware of their existence. It has been a traumatic week to witness what started as an issue of reservation turning into a bloody caste conflict, between the *Gujjars* and the *Meenas*, over the former's demand for inclusion into the scheduled tribe list in Rajasthan State.

The *Meenas* or minas, the community that is now arraigned against the *Gujjars* getting the ST status have an interesting history. Unlike the *Gujjars* who are spread out in north-western India, *Meenas* are a tribe found only in Rajasthan. A land-owning class in the ancient *Matsya* (modern Rajasthan) and were even seen as *kshatriyas*, like the *Gujjars* in the earlier times. However, their origin is still not clear as historians differ about whether they had a Central Asian origin like the *Gujjars* or are an indigenous community.[2]

Like the *Gujjars*, the British found *Meenas* also as a thorn in their flesh, and one British chronicler even called them "revengeful and blood thirsty". This community was denominated as a criminal tribe. It may be seen that both *Gujjars* and the *Meenas* who belonged to a much higher caste order were relegated into criminal tribes during the British times. However, post-independence *Meenas*, who are economically better off, being landowners, were classified in the 1960s as a scheduled tribe, while the economically inferior *Gujjars* atleast in Rajasthan, got the OBC status.[3]

The *Gujjars* were quite reconciled to this status, after their demand in the seventies to be included in the ST category had been rejected. However, their problem began in the late nineties when the NDA government led by the BJP with an eye on the Jat votes in Rajasthan, before the 1998 elections to the Assembly promised them an OBC status. When this promise was fulfilled in 1999, the *Gujjars* suddenly found themselves at a disadvantage as the more economically and socially as well educationally powerful *Jats* started cornering the OBC share.

Again the BJP came into the picture and in the run-up to the July 17th, 2003 Assembly polls, its Chief Minister Vasundhara Raje Scindia promised the *Gujjars* that if she came to power, she would recommend their inclusion in the ST list to the Centre. It is this unfulfilled demand, which has erupted into violence, unrest and caste clashes, in Rajasthan and spread to Delhi, Uttar Pradesh and Haryana also.

In Rajasthan, the seats reserved for Scheduled Tribes are expected to go up, and one of the major casualties will be the Dausa Lok Sabha seat, considered as the only gujjar stronghold. A seat represented by late Rajesh Pilot for long and now held by his son Sachin, it is likely to be reserved for Scheduled Tribes. Similarly, a few Assembly seats held by the *Gujjars* are also likely to face extinction, as far as the *Gujjars* are concerned. It is this lurking fear which has also ignited the kind of rage among the *Gujjars*. The resistance of the *Meenas* for the inclusion in the Scheduled Tribe list is directly related to their apprehension that their almost unchallenged dominance of this category will be a thing of the past, if the *Gujjars*, enter the list.

One suggestion to overcome this dangerous deadlock is to categories the OBCs like in Karnataka and Kerala, and creates a quota within the quota. This may solve the problem when it comes to sharing seats in education and jobs; however, this is unlikely to allay the apprehensions of the *Gujjars* about the political loss they would suffer, following the fresh delimitation process. It is imperative in such a complicated situation that all political parties put their heads together and find an amicable solution to this crisis.[4]

Dr. Javaid Rahi, Secretary, Tribal Foundation said that the main objective of launching this unprecedented movement is to channelise the energies of *Gujjar* Backward youth of the State through proper guidance enabling them to compete in different competitive exams by making a mark of positive contribution to the State in particular and to the country in general. He said in initial phase of the movement we have to reach out to at least 20 to 30 thousand youths of the community who are presently pursuing various academic and professional degree courses in various colleges and universities of the State to harness their skills, develop their personality and improve their communication skills and to prepare and to equip them well for the challenges facing them ahead. He further said that the movement is an attempt to reach out to the marginalised, neglected and educationally suppressed youth of the society mainly Gujjar-Bakerwal to equip themselves well with educational capabilities, cultural sensitisation and social awareness.

Dr. Rahi said that those of the community who have already created a niche in their lives including Dr. Shahid Iqbal IAS, Suleman Chowdhary IPS, Ch. Ayaz Kohli IAS and other IAS officers will share their experiences with tribal youth and streamline the capabilities of the younger generation of the community during interaction programmes under the movements. There are various agencies that are cooperating with the foundation for the smooth and successful conduct of the movement, including Centre for Life Long Learning, University of Jammu, Jammu and Kashmir Gujjar Bakerwal Students Federation, SC/ST Student Federation and other local organisations. The Tribal Foundation during interactions will provide basic knowledge about different schemes run by different Government/semi-government departments for Scheduled Tribes youth, and provide co-ordination to Gujjar NGOs' / *Bhawans* across the country including those who are working for *Gujjars* in Punjab, HP, Haryana, Rajasthan, Delhi, Gujrat, Uthar Pradesh, Uttaranchal willing to provide financial assistance to poor students belonging to Gujjar Bakerwal of the State for all types of studies up-to Ph.D., level. *Dr. Rahi* said "we have already requested the State Governor *N.N Vohra*, Chief Minister *Omar Abdullah* and *Gujjar* Ministers for help and also wrote to different colleges, universities of the State for their coordination and guidance to make the movement a success". Others who spoke include *Ch. Haq Nawaz,* President

SC /ST Student Union, *Sheraz Bajad,* Jammu and Kashmir Tribal Student Union and *Ch Zulikarnain Bajran.*[5]

Gujjar agitation for Reorganisation as Scheduled Tribe in Rajasthan

Coupled with aggressive campaigns in the Scheduled Tribe belt, the BJP won major dividends in the 2003 Assembly elections;[6] it secured 120 seats, winning the majority of the 28 reserved seats, unprecedented in the history of the party. Six of the eight Gujjar legislators belonged to the BJP. Clearly, the Gujjar base had begun to shift from the Congress to the BJP. But compared to *Meenas, Gujjars* appear to be politically dispensable. According to Yashvir Singh, former general secretary of the Gujjar Mahasabha, it was during the time of the Ashok Gehlot-led Congress government that the demand for inclusion in the Scheduled Tribe category was reiterated by the *Gujjars*. The demand was first made in 1984 when Shiv Charan Mathur was Chief Minister. He rejected the proposal. Vasudev Sharma, State secretary of the Communist Party of India (Marxist), told *Frontline* that the issue now was much more than the crisis facing a particular government or a particular individual. The entire State had the potential to get engulfed in the caste cauldron owing to the mishandling of the situation by the government and the politics of caste populism played by the BJP.

At the all-party meeting held on May 31, 2003, the Chief Minister *Vasundhara Raje* demanded that the opposition to condemn the violence, which it turned down. At the meeting, she disclosed that a report submitted by 26 District Collectors on the status of *Gujjars* was not in favour of including the community in the Scheduled Tribe category. Despite several rounds of discussion with political parties, the State government, and the Chief Minister in particular, continued to be non-committal, leaving the issue in a state of limbo. This was one of the reasons why an appeal for peace by all political parties failed to produce the desired impact.[7] On June 1, 2003, fearful of a *Meena* reprisal against her government with *Meena* legislators threatening to resign, the Chief Minister began consultations with a section of the *Meena* leadership, even as representatives of the Gujjar movement were waiting to hear from her. Minister for Food and Civil Supplies *Kirori Lal Meena* declared his Opposition to conferring Scheduled Tribe status on *Gujjars*. Even as *Gujjars* continued with their agitation and the *Akhil Bharatiya Gujjar Mahasabha* threw its weight behind the movement, the influential *Meena* community, fearing a dilution of the Scheduled Tribe quota, decided to "liberate" the blocked national highways.[8]

Naresh Meena, a Congress youth leader, told that the issue was no longer one of the Congress or the BJP but concerned the "*samaj*" or the community of *Meenas*. He decided to support the BJP legislators belonging to the *Meena* community and floated the *Adivasi Meen Sena* (the term *Meen* is derived from the *Meena* deity, *Meenesh*). He clarified that this was not only a force of *Meenas* but of all Scheduled Tribes in the State. He said that he was prepared to quit the Congress if the party did not take into account the interests of the *Meenas*. "Why do they want Scheduled Tribe status? I think they want to be politically influential so that they can rally the other tribes against us," he said about the *Gujjars* agitation. He stressed that the *Gujjars* were not making the demand for their economic upliftment. Sensing the *Meenas*' anger, the Congress has been rather silent over the reservation issue, preferring to criticise the government on the police action.[9]

The *Gujjars* maintain that they qualify for Scheduled Tribe status in every manner. According to *Yashvir Singh*, in 1857 the British branded the *Gujjars* as a criminal tribe as the community had taken cudgels against the colonial rulers. In 1924, under the Criminal Tribes Act, *Gujjars* and other tribes designated as criminal tribes were subject to strict regulations. In 1951, *Sardar Vallabbhai* Patel got the Act repealed. *Gujjars* figured were among the Backward Castes in 1981. Subsequently, in 1993, the community was included in the list of OBCs. *Yashvir Singh* said: "We cohabit the same environment as the Scheduled Tribes in most parts of Rajasthan. We are landless, we earn a living by grazing cattle, we are economically and educationally backward and there is not a single officer from among us in the Indian Administrative Service. Culturally too, we fulfill the requirements [for classification as a Scheduled Tribe]." *Anna Patil*, national president of the *Gujjar Mahasabha,* appealed to the media to keep the *Meenas* out of the picture. "We are not talking about the *Meenas* here. We are talking about us. Please focus on that."[10]

According to Census 2001, of the 12 tribes scheduled for the State, *Meenas* (spelt as Mina in the Census) are the most populous tribe, comprising nearly 53.5 per cent of the total Scheduled Tribe population followed by *Bhils*. Together, the *Meenas* and *Bhils* constitute 93 per cent of the Scheduled Tribe population, while *Garasias, Damords, Dhankads* and *Saharias* comprise 6.6 per cent, and six other tribes, including Bhil *Meenas*, constitute the residual 0.3 per cent. *Meenas* mostly inhabit *Dhaulpur, Bharatpur, Sawai Madhopur, Karauli and Dausa* districts. They also comprise more than 90 per cent of the tribal population in *Alwar, Jhunjhunu, Sikar, Tonk* and *Churu* districts. Employment and educational levels are much higher among *Meenas* compared with the other groups. Seventy- eight caste groups, including *Gujjars*, figure in the Backward Classes category in the State.[11]

A fresh *Gujjar*s agitation in Ajmer has been called on March 24th 2010. It is claimed by the Gujjar leaders that at least two lakh *Gujjars* will join the protest. The railway administration is on the alert and has demanded extra force to safeguard the tracks.[12]

Gujjars, who have been on stir demanding 5 per cent reservation for them and three other Special Backward Classes (SBCs) in jobs and education, called off their agitation on 5th January, 2011 night. Their decision came after a final round of talks between a group of Ministers and *Kirori Singh Bainsla*, who spearheaded the agitation.

Unlike in the past, the agitation did not witness any violence. It, however, affected rail and road traffic in east Rajasthan, in the 2007-08 years, *Gujjar* agitation claimed 70 lives in police firing during the BJP government.[13]

The final round of talks on January 5th 2011 focused on the issue of 5 per cent reservation and demand for withdrawal of cases against *Gujjars*. The other aspects, involving over 10 demands including those pertaining to the ambit of the Devnarain Board set up for focused development of the *Gujjar* areas, jobs for the children of those killed in police firing and disability certificates to those maimed in the agitation, were agreed upon in the initial rounds of talks between a 51-member *Gujjar* delegation and Ministers.

The agreement, signed between the government and the *Gujjar* leaders in the chamber of Chief Secretary *S. Ahmed*, provides six months to the government to assess the status of the communities in the OBC. The Rajasthan High Court, ruling on a petition challenging 5 per cent reservation for these communities, had asked the government to justify the quota with the supporting data. The court also suspended implementation of the new legislation on quota, passed during the previous regime, for a year. *Col. Bainsla* met Chief Minister *Ashok Gehlot* at the end of the talks late in the evening and asked him for the "cooperation".

The truce allows continuation of the current recruitment process for inducting about one lakh government employees the move in fact triggered the current agitation by the *Gehlot* government. The government promised to file a review petition before the High Court on the 4 per cent reservation out of the promised 5 per cent one per cent is to be given in the current recruitment as well reportedly citing the court order in the case of *Joshi vs Karnataka* government.[14]

Conclusion

As part of their agitation, the *Gujjars* went on blocking the National Highways paralysing the traffic, setting fire to road ways bus railway lines, police stations and government offices, causing losses to the tune of hundreds of crores of rupees. The government under BJP had to take to firing on the masses killing seventy people.

At last, after rounds of talks on January 6th 2011, the government of Congress with the *Gujjar* leader agreed upon to allow the 5 per cent of reservation to *Gujjars* in jobs along with other comforts to mitigate the grievances faced during the agitations.[15] The *Gujjars* had to face the anger of the *Meenas* while fighting for their demand for inclusion in Scheduled Tribes because of the fear of the *Meenas* to lose their share in scheduled tribe quota if the *Gujjars* are also allowed into the same scheduled tribe band.

References

1. Nau Nihal Singh (2003). *The royal Gurjars: their contribution*, Anmol Publications, LTD. pp. 329-330
2. P.K. Mohanty (2006). *Encyclopaedia of Scheduled Tribes in India 5 Vol. Set.* Gyan Publishing House, pp. 184-185.
3. Hari Shanker Sharma, Mohan Lal Sharma (1992). *Geographical facets of Rajasthan*. Kuldeep Publications, p. 262.
4. Jeremy Page (30 May 2008). "India's Gujjar caste fights for a downgrade." *The Times of India*.
5. *Raising Kashmir*, Daily, 19 Dec. 2010.
6. 2003 Assembly Elections Rajasthan, ECI, Government of India, India.
7. *The Hindu*, Daily, Rajasthan, 1st June, 2003.
8. *Indian Express*, Daily, Rajasthan, June 2nd, 2003.
9. *Times of India*, daily, Rajasthan, June 15th, 2003.
10. Meena Radhakrishna, "Dishonored by history". *Folio: Special issue with the Sunday Magazine. The Hindu*. 16th 2006.

11. Documents of Census of India, Government of India, India, 2001.
12. *The Hindu*, Daily, March 25th 2010.
13. *Times of India*, Daily, 5th January, 2011.
14. *Indian Express*, Daily,6th January, 2011
15. *Times of India*, Daily, 7th January, 2011.

INDEX